HOME INSPECTION GUIDE

How to tell if a "Bargain" is *Really* a Bargain and
How to Spot Expensive Repairs *Before* You Buy

By

JOHN ANDERSON

FIRST EDITION © 1992 BROUGHTON HALL INC.

ISBN-0934748-43-8

Manufactured in the United States of America

TABLE OF CONTENTS

ILLUSTRATIONS

APPENDICES

1.0   A HOME OF YOUR OWN

A home of your own. It's the cornerstone of the American dream. And it's also possible. Even with skyrocketing house prices, many people can afford a house, whether they think they can or not.

One part of finding an affordable home involves knowing the intricacies of financing and the legal side of things, and those issues are dealt with in a companion publication by Broughton Hall, *FINDING A BARGAIN HOME*. Another part of finding a home that is right for you, the part we deal with in this book, concerns the practical tasks of finding a good, solid house that is not going to surprise you with hefty bills for problems you had not suspected, or how to estimate accurately the costs to improve a fixer upper. This is not as difficult as most people think, but you must know what to look for. This book shows you, step by step, how to give a house a thorough once-over so that you can recognize the best of the bargains.

If money was no object, of course, you wouldn't need a book like this. You could build new; you could afford to have problems fixed, even if they were unexpected; and you could call in a professional inspector to look at every house that interested you, however slightly.

For most of us, though, money is **not** unlimited. Even if we could afford to have houses built to our specifications, many of us might prefer to live in an older property; character, location, period charm, or other considerations will often outweigh the attractions of even the newest buildings. We set a budget, and somehow we have to stay inside that budget — which means that any defects in the house have to be reflected in a lower purchase price.

Nor can we afford to pay several hundred dollars to an inspector just to find out what a house is like. Rather, we need to be able to check for ourselves that the house we are after is in good enough condition to warrant hiring an inspector. Only then do we spend the money on a professional inspection.

Now, you are unlikely to be as naive as one girl I used to work with. She saw an apartment in a charming old building, fell in love with it, and only on the pressing advice of her friends (me among them) did she agree to hire an inspector.

On the appointed day he met her outside the building — she had the key — and they went inside to look the place over. They had already discussed her requirements and budget, so he knew (or thought he knew) that she was being realistic.

She opened the door for him and ushered him in: she was already thinking of it as "her" place. She was somewhat surprised when, instead of examining anything closely, he looked into each room in turn, peeked into a couple of closets, and finally said, "Look. It wouldn't be fair to charge you a full inspection price for this. Take my advice: don't touch it with a long pole. If you want a written report, I'll do it, but that will cost you the full price. Call it forty bucks to cover my time in coming out here, and forget it."

She was aghast. "Can you just *tell* me a bit about it?" she asked.

He glanced at his watch. "Well, very briefly, you've got wet rot and dry rot; I'm not sure, but I think there are beetles in the rafters; that wall over there"— he pointed — "needs replastering, and I think the moisture that's spoiling it is because you need the lead flashing renewed, which is a very expensive job indeed; some of these old houses have internal gutters, and you have to take the house half apart to fix them. You've got lead pipes, which I would want to have replaced with copper if you don't want lead poisoning from drinking the water, and there's been a steady dropping leak by the bath which has probably left the floor so weak that the people downstairs are lucky they don't have your bath in their kitchen. Is that enough, or do you want it in writing?"

She gave him the forty dollars.

If she had known what she was doing — and especially if she had used the checklists in this book — she could have discovered all of those problems, and probably the rest of the drawbacks that he didn't bother to tell her about. And she was lucky: he was dead straight about it, and told her what the problems were and passed on the money that he saved by not making a full report. He could, after all, have charged her the full $200.

If she had *not* had an inspector, and *not* used a book like this, she could have been in very real trouble: out at least thousands, and possibly tens of thousands, of dollars. When I discussed this with another inspector, thousands of miles from the first one, he told me an almost identical story; he had just surveyed a house which was so far out of compliance with the building codes (especially with respect to electrical installations) that it was a death-trap. Rather than charge his client the full fee ($200), he offered to do a one-page report which said, in effect, that the house was not worth considering in its present state for *any* money, and only to charge $100. In this case, a written statement was essential because the deal was already in escrow, and the buyer (the inspector's client) had made his offer "subject to inspection."

The seller was furious and threatened to sue the inspector. The inspector shrugged. "Sue me," he said. "I know who's going to win. And I'll counter-sue for harassment, and then you'll have to pay for that as well as for bringing the house into conformity with the building codes." He was never sued.

Unfortunately, not all the people who advertise themselves as building inspectors are fully qualified; in many states, there is little or no regulation, and no bonding. This is another reason, though, why this book is so invaluable. If it is clear that you know more about building inspection than the "building inspector" (and you will know a lot about building inspection by the time you finish this book), you will know that you are not dealing with a trustworthy character. And if you *are* dealing with a trustworthy inspector, of course, understanding the nature of building inspection will help you to understand his report. A qualified building inspector will respect you more if he knows that *you* know what you are talking about.

How do you find a building inspector? The best way, as usual, is by personal recommendation — though watch out for an inspector who is recommended by the seller of the house you want to have inspected! Look for an I.C.B.O. number on his letterhead (this stands for the International Conference of Building Officials, and is probably the most rigorous of all available qualifications), or just discuss your requirements over the phone. A good inspector won't try to blind you with science, and he (or she) won't evade your questions. Once you have read this book, you should be able to distinguish between a good inspector and a bad one — and you should need one soon, because this book shows you the way to find the house *you* want.

1.1   HOW MUCH HOUSE DO YOU NEED?

One of the first questions to ask yourself is how much house you need. There are two different schools of thought here. One buys for the future, for the long term. The other argues that with real-estate prices constantly on the rise, you can afford to move as often as you like — even every year or two, if you make the right deals — and make a profit every time.

I must confess that I am of the first school. I *hate* moving, and I suspect that most other people do, too. Unless you are one of those people who settles very lightly upon a house, like a butterfly on a flower, it takes a while to get your house the way *you* want it. That desk, which fits so perfectly in that corner — where can you put it in the new house? Where are you going to put all the bookshelves? Is there a convenient and secure place for the china cabinet? If there are stairs, and you have toddlers, you will have to look at safety gates; if you like lots of light, and the previous owners subscribed to the "low and romantic" school of lighting, you will need to work out how to install new fixtures, or buy lots more standard and end table lamps. Each of us has his or own requirements, and it is foolish not to try to meet them as nearly as possible. This is, after all, one of the many things that distinguishes a home form a house.

If you are like me, you will therefore want to look to the future. Do you have children? Do you plan to have children? Or are your children growing up and leaving home? How many rooms do you actually need? Don't imagine that your needs are the same as other people's, even if their lifestyle looks similar to yours. My wife and I, who have no children, reckon that the optimum number of rooms for us is five, all fairly small: a bedroom, a living room, my study, her study/workroom (which doubles as guest bedroom — she's tidier than I am) and a storeroom we can use as a darkroom. The reason for wanting small rooms is that it makes for a smaller house, which is cheaper and easier to maintain.

Your needs are almost certainly different, unless (like us) there are only two of you and you both work at home. But our example gives you a good basis for working out what sort of accommodation *you* might need to suit *your* lifestyle.

Be realistic, too. A big garden may look beautiful when you first inspect the house. How much work does it take, though? If the present owner is retired, and the garden is his principal hobby, it may take far more time that you can afford to keep it in enjoyable condition. Do you *need* a two-car garage? Come to that, do you need a garage at all? In some areas, parking on the street can save you thousands of dollars, compared with buying a house with a garage. Though if you're like most people, you probably need the garage for storage space worse than you need it as a place to park the car!

Of course, if you are into "fixer-uppers" which you can sell at a handsome profit (Section 1.4), or if you simply believe in moving frequently, you can afford to be more casual about all these questions: if you don't like it, it's not for long anyway, and you just move. *In general*, though, you can reckon that it will take at least six months to a year before you can show a real profit on a house (taking into account finance costs, inspection costs and the rest, as well as the purchase price), and it can easily take two years. Realistically, therefore, you should not expect to move more than every three to five years, even if you are a "rolling stone."

Expenses

Other things being equal, a bigger house means bigger expenses: higher property taxes, high maintenance costs, higher utility bills, more money out of your pocket. Bear this in mind when you are planning your move. Until you own a house, you may not even realize the number of different charges that you can find in your mailbox: water, sewage, electricity, garbage collection, and more.

Also, watch out for charges that you may not even have though of. In about 1983 I was thinking of buying a flat in London. It was available at a very attractive price, in a location that I very much liked — Chelsea, on the King's Road. There was a doorman, and daily garbage collection, and all kinds of good things. Then I found out what the services charge was (over and above the "regular" cost of the flat): almost $2000 *per year*. **That's $150 a month!** Obviously, someone had to pay for that doorman and all the other facilities, but I hadn't realized quite how much they would cost.

All right, that was London. But much the same could happen in New York, and the same story could be told on a lesser scale about any number of other cities. Don't be afraid to ask someone, "What are your expenses?" They may well understate them, saying that an electricity bill which averages $100 a month is "usually under $100" or that garbage collection is "a couple of bucks a week" when it's $2.95; but keep your ears open for whole *categories* of expenses that you might not have thought of, like the $2000 service charge.

1.2   <u>LOCATION</u>

There is an old saying in the real estate business that the three most important considerations in real estate are location, location and location. This is best illustrated by considering the *best* house in the *worst* area of town, and the *worst* house in the *best* area of town.

In the bad area, the fear is always that the one good house will be dragged down to the general level of the rest. If keeping up the standards is an uphill struggle, it is too easy to let things slide. In the extreme, if there are broken-down cars in the front yards and bicycles tires in all the threes, the good house is seen as a besieged bastion of respectability in a slum area, and the smart buyer will not touch it with a ten-foot pole.

In the good area, on the other hand, it is *very easy* to bring the bad house up to the standard of the others — and when you do, its value will skyrocket. Fortunately for the smart housebuyer — that's you — most people can't see beyond the missing boards on the picket fence, the need for a good coat of paint, and the general air of dilapidation. Of course, if there are *structural* problems, that's another matter (and one which should bring the price of the house down even further), but your eyes should light up at the sight of a slightly neglected house in a good area.

<u>Site</u> — Strictly, site is not the same as location — but it can be just as important. For example, a house in a low-lying area may be prone to flooding; and even if it is not prone to flooding, the water

table may be so near the surface that it would be impossible to dig a cellar. After all, well-diggers rely on getting down to the water table to replenish the well — and a cellar can be embarrassingly like a large well, if it is dug in the wrong place.

Look out for steep slopes which may be subject to mud slides, or for large areas of dry vegetation which are an invitation to a brush fire. Californians are particularly cavalier about the location of their houses: there are some, worth many millions of dollars, which are completely uninsurable because of the *double* risk of mud-slides and brush fires. In another place I looked at once, the back yard was eroding at a frightening rate: there were big cracks and washouts within ten or fifteen feet of the house, and you could see daylight under the back fence when you looked *downward*. The house was built on a mesa, and the mesa was getting smaller all the time, so there was about a ten-foot drop at the back fence.

Trees are pretty, but you had better be sure they are stable, too: a couple of tons of tree hitting your house on a windy night will assuredly get your attention. If the trees are a part of the house lot, trim them as necessary: if they are someone else's, put him on notice that you expect him to trim them, and if he does not, you will have them trimmed yourself. Also, remember that big trees have big roots — roots that can snake under your property, lift your pathways, crack your foundations, and block your drains. Be wary, too, of young but established trees growing too near the house: when they get larger in diameter, will they grow into and damage the roof or other overhangs of the house?

Watch for streams: a brook at the foot of the garden is very attractive, but what happens in the rainy season? Does it flood your cellar?

Marsh is another drawback, and so is sand: a beach-front home is no fun when every wind fills everything in the house with sand. Do not be blinded by the natural (or even man-made) beauty of a site. Ask yourself why nobody ever built there before.

"Gentrification"

To return to location, there is one possible exception to the "good area" rule, and that is the "rising area."

In the nature of things, the desirability of different areas rises and falls. A new road can raise or lower property values; an economic boom or a slump can also have an effect. There are fashions, too, which may be sparked by one smart buyer: *someone* must have been the first to see the potential in New York's run-down SoHo. There may even be deliberate civic regeneration policies, sometimes with attractive financial help, but unless these catch the imagination of the right people, they can be risky.

The advantage of a "gentrified" area are obvious: the values of your property can skyrocket. A friend-of-a-friend really cleaned up on this one. She bought a sound house *very* cheaply, because it was in an area that was scheduled for redevelopment and it seemed almost certain that the house would be knocked down in three to five years. Then, in one of those extraordinary switches of policy that characterize local government, the redevelopment was cancelled; the street, which was serving as a "rat run" for local commuters, was sealed off at one end; and the whole area was designated as an urban conservation area! The value of the house went up by a factor of five in a few days, and by the time she sold it (only two years later) it was worth more than *twenty times* what she had paid for it!

While bargains like that are hard to come by, you can still do very well out of "gentrification" if you are prepared to do two things.

One is to fit in with your new neighbors. The kind of yuppies who often "gentrify" areas are sometimes rather wearing neighbors. Slaves to the work ethic, they work the kind of hours that would give nightmares to a 19th-century immigrant in an East Side sweat shop, and the only way that they can unload the money they earn is on their houses and their possessions. If you feel that you would be unhappy parking your beat-up old Chrysler among all the BMWs, or trying to buy a decent piece of beef in a shop that specialized in radiccio, you might do better to avoid such an area — or buy a BMW and change your diet! Of course, if you *are* a yuppie, "please disregard the above notice."

The other consideration with "gentrification" is that until the area is fully "gentrified," you are effectively living in the middle of a building site. This can be noisy, dusty, dirty and even hazardous; you have to be careful on broken sidewalks, and unduly adventurous children can get into serious trouble with construction machinery and gutted, floorboardless buildings.

If this isn't a worry to you, great. There is only one other problem, which is a "what if", namely: "What if the gentrification doesn't succeed?" In that case, you can be left with an overpriced house in a poor section of town, exactly the kind of thing I warned about above. Generally, though, gentrification *does* succeed, largely because the best gentrification plans are not plans at all; they are grass-roots movements by people with good sense, who are willing to put their money where their mouths are.

If someone tries to persuade that you that an area is "ripe" for gentrification, on the other hand, this could simply mean that it is run down, and they are trying to persuade you that the house is worth more than it is. How early you get into a gentrification area will depend on your "nose" for gentrification: I have known some people who were the first or second kids on the block, two or three times in a row, "traded up" each time, and ended up in truly gorgeous houses.

Some Things to Look Out For

If you have children, you may want to check out the reputation of the local school system, and how easy it will be for them to get to school. If you do not have children, you may find that schools make noisy neighbors.

Other neighbors worth looking out for are all-night convenience stores (which are convenient, but invite a constant stream of traffic); police stations (generally good for security); shops of all kinds; and (using the term "neighbors" loosely) cemeteries. For some reason, houses that overlook cemeteries are often obtainable at much lower prices than houses with a more cheerful view, despite the fact that you could hardly wish for quieter neighbors and the land is likely to remain undeveloped.

If public transportation is important to you, check out the buses, train stations and airports — and remember that all three can be a mixed blessing, especially if you are on the flight path of a major airport or if the midnight train rattles the cups on the shelf. A *good* local map can be a worthwhile investment, once you have narrowed down the area in which you wish to live.

1.3   OLD OR NEW?

Almost by definition, this book is not aimed at the buyer of a brand-new house. If a house is literally newly built, most of the problems that this book will help you to spot are unlikely to exist — and if they do, they should be covered by some kind of warranty. On the other hand, there are a few builders (or more often, subcontractors) who pull some horrific tricks on new homes; one of the most common is running out of wood of the right size and the "cobbling together" of two smaller pieces which should have been one continuous piece of wood. When the piece of wood in question is a roof beam, this can be hair-raising! Such tricks are, fortunately, very rare indeed, but they do happen.

There is also the question of whether you want to buy *older* or *newer* property. Some of the newest stuff, even in expensive houses, is not very well put together. A while back, I was admiring one new house in Southern California, which looked very nice indeed and cost something like $195,000. A friend's mother happened to live in the same development, and I asked her what the houses were made of: I had assumed they were the usual Californian timber frame construction. Her answer was less technical, but no less telling. "Spit and hope," she said.

Depending on where you are looking at a house, the difference between "spit and hope," well-made frame houses, and other forms of construction such as brick (or cinder-block) or reinforced concrete or even adobe can be a factor influencing your choice. Apart from availability, this is partly a matter of personal preference and partly a matter of practicality. For example, up in California's Gold Country, there are brick houses which do not meet modern earthquake regulations but which have, nevertheless, been standing now for a hundred years or more. The fact that these buildings are "out of code" may well make some people very nervous; others won't worry a bit.

My personal preference is for older property: for many years, I lived in a brick-built house, and I prefer the solidity and sound installation of this sort of construction. It also required very little maintenance, though when it did require maintenance, it was expensive. It was well insulated and very cosy despite being in a considerably colder climate than California's. Now I live in a "spit and hope" house, which is very much more conveniently laid out (more electrical outlets, low-maintenance light alloy windows, bigger closets, and a much lighter, airier feel), but I miss the brick whenever I think of attaching something (like bookshelves) to the walls. Also, I find that the new house lacks that indefinable something that we call "character."

In the rest of this book, I have tried to keep my personal preferences to a minimum, and to make it clear whenever they surface; but I thought it would make it very much easier for you, the reader, to know "where I'm coming from," as we say in California.

1.4   FIXED OR FIXER-UPPER?

My European friends can't believe how little work is usually required for an American "fixer-upper." Countless of my English friends have replaced floors, roofs and window frames; and I knew someone who lived in Italy who was having trouble with the drains, which had been installed *seventeen hundred* years ago in late Roman times. In this country, though, a "fixer-upper" normally means just a coat of paint and some new carpets; at worst, it rarely means more than a house that needs paint, carpets, a couple of cracked windows replaced, and a new kitchen and bathroom(s). Work which costs a couple of thousand dollars can add $10,000 or more to the value of a house. Why? How come the seller doesn't spend that $2,000 and earn a cool $8,000 profit?

The answer is, of course, that many times they do — and if you buy a house with a new "dream kitchen," you are the person they earn it from! But there are several reasons why a house can become a "fixer upper" and remain that way until you buy it — at a very good price!

These reasons are discussed in the next section, but it is worth enumerating the advantages of a "fixer-upper." Not only do you save money, you also have the enormous advantage that you can "customize" your house, the way *you* want it. You want gas burners for boiling and frying, and an electric oven? No problem, if the place has to be fixed up anyway. But if it's already been fixed up, you're not going to want to tear out the gas oven to install an electric one. You want fire-engine red carpets? Fine (but consider the impact when you come to sell the house). You want one room lined with bookshelves, or a lathe in the garage? All of this is much easier if you have a "fixer-upper" to start with.

Reasons Why Houses Deteriorate

Two main reasons that houses become "fixer-uppers" are (1) money and (2) creeping neglect, often as a result of indifference or unawareness.

For all sorts of reasons, people don't have the money to keep up their houses. Maybe they are young, and not too good at budgeting. Maybe they are well past retirement age, and are living on a very modest income. Maybe they are in their prime, but they've been laid off and have been unable to find work that pays as well as they were accustomed to. Maybe they have young children who are turning out to be a far greater expense than their parents had expected, and who are also doing nothing to improve the value of the house. People of all sorts, ages and conditions can find that they can't afford to maintain their houses.

By buying houses like these at bargain prices, you are, in a very real way, helping people get out from what has turned out to be a crushing financial commitment; and if you can afford the house, you are getting what you want, and they are getting what they need.

The other main reason that houses become "fixer-uppers", the scenario that I have called "creeping neglect" or indifference, comes about when there are people who genuinely don't care about living in a shabby or old-fashioned accommodation. As long as the place is clean and doesn't smell funny, they just don't notice that paint is getting rubbed and marred, or that carpets have the occasional hole; a throw rug covers the hole, and that is the closest they ever get to maintenance.

Another neglect/indifference problem arises with the *partially completed renovation*. When "don't-care" homeowners finally bestir themselves, they may well do half the work (often the difficult half) and then run out of interest or enthusiasm when the woodwork is stripped and the windows are replaced and the old carpets are taken out. If you can buy at this stage, you may be able to get a truly excellent deal, with the benefit of a reduced price *and* half the renovation done for you!

Or again, the deterioration may be very gradual, so that the old owners do not really notice. Maybe they bought the house in the 1950s, and put in all the latest fashions and labor-saving devices — and then "froze" in a sort of time-warp, doing little or nothing since. They may be traditionally house-proud, and very careful, so everything survives in amazingly good condition; but if the decor and the kitchen and everything else are museum pieces, and if the house has been lived in for thirty or forty years, you still have a "fixer upper" on your hands. As a bonus, you can often get remarkably good prices for 1950s refrigerators and other "retro" fittings.

And these are only the most usual scenarios: there are others. I have known some people, well-to-do professionals, who have moved from one part of the country to another and loaned their houses to their children. That way, they thought, they would be getting a triple benefit: continued capital appreciation on the home, the tax shelter associated with first and second homes, and a helping hand for the children. Unfortunately, the kids ("kids" in their thirties in one case!) trashed the house so badly that the only way to sell it was as a "fixer-upper." The parents still had massive capital appreciation — they had often seen their houses appreciate by ten or twenty times over two or three decades — and they were freed of the hassle of supervising clean-up work.

14

Is a Fixer-Upper for You?

From what I have already said, it is clear that "fixer-uppers" represent the very best value in housing — but it should also be clear that they are not for everyone. While *most* people will get tremendous value out of fixer-uppers, there are four types of people who should think hard before buying one:

"Don't-Care" Homebuyers — If you genuinely don't care too much about living in the latest and most fashionable surroundings, it's nothing to be ashamed of. Indeed, you could make a strong case that this is the only responsible, "save-the-world" attitude: if you can live with things that are out of date, and with decor that is past its prime, you are saving the earth's valuable resources.

The drawback to this approach, however, is that if you buy a house that is *already* a fixer-upper, there is a risk that it will continue to deteriorate — and if it does, you might end up with a house that requires more than just cosmetic attention. "Eternal vigilance is the price of freedom," runs the old slogan; and constant vigilance is also necessary to make sure that your house doesn't go over the edge, from a fixer-upper to a basket case.

Of course, if you check the structure periodically (using this book), you will be well placed to spot any deterioration, even if you are a "don't-care" type. To be quite honest, that is the sort of person I am: a trip to Europe or a new camera always takes precedence over a new carpet!

Homebuyers who are short of money — We're all short of money, even the few millionaires I know. There's a difference, though, between not being able to afford *everything* you want, and not being able to afford *anything* you want. If you are really, seriously short of money, and the house purchase is going to stretch your budget to the limits, the **only** sort of fixer-upper you should even begin to consider is one that needs a bare minimum of paint and cleaning-up. If there are any more serious faults (such as insect infestation), and if you cannot afford to have them fixed immediately, the house can rapidly deteriorate to the point where it is worth much, much less than you paid for it. This is why careful inspection is *essential*.

Even if the fixing-up that is required is minor, you must take into account how it will affect you. Some people can cheerfully "camp" in a place that is all but falling down about their ears, while others will throw conniptious fits at having to live in such surroundings. The real problems here can arise when a couple with seriously different expectations buy a fixer-upper. He may be happy enough, while she complains at living in a slum; or she may be able to concentrate on the renovation in an orderly, step-by-step way while he has unrealistic expectations of finding the house in apple-pie order with his slippers warming by the fire and dinner waiting for him when he gets home. He may want to spend a limited budget on a new hi-fi, while she points out that the money would be better spent on re-fencing the yard; or **he** may want to re-fence the yard while **she** wants new furniture. If you are buying as a couple (or even with a friend), then discuss it *thoroughly* first.

People who work at home — If you work at home, the disruption of working on a fixer-upper can be altogether too much. This is true whether you work for profit (running a typing service, dressmaking, towing service) or as a housewife/househusband. Trying to fit a renovation around other commitments can be altogether too much like hard work, and (like the previous category) it may also place more strain on a relationship than you feel that either of you can comfortably handle.

People with young children — A house that is being renovated can be a very dangerous "adventure playground" for young children. Paint strippers; splintery wood and sharp nails; missing floorboards or guardrails — do you really want to take those risks? Even where they damage is not serious, it may not be much fun: I am told that when I was about five, I was fascinated by "Seraphite" — a hard stopper used for filling cracked plaster. Our next-door-neighbor was renovating his house, and when he reached for his pipe for a soothing draught of tobacco, he was not pleased to find that I had carefully filled it some hours earlier, so that it was now filled with hard, pink stone!

One More Advantage of a Fixer-Upper

There is, however, one more advantage of a fixer-upper that I have not yet mentioned. It is that, for the most part, faults have not been covered up. Is that sparkling new paint job to cover up a stain from a leaky roof? A leaky roof that is alright now, in the summer, but which will come back to haunt you when the rains come? Is that beautiful new kitchen meant to make you fall in love with the place and distract you from the fact that the wiring is more suitable for a Fourth of July fireworks display than for actually running domestic appliances?

It is true that *very occasionally* a seller will leave a number of obvious, minor faults with the intention of distracting you from bigger and more serious faults. It's unusual, but it has been known to happen.

Of course, none of these tricks (or attempted tricks) will affect you anyway; after all, if you use the systematic approach that is laid down in this book, you *will* see the problems. If there are any.

1.5   BUILDING CODES

One thing which I thought would be as well to deal with as soon as possible is the question of building codes. These fall into two groups. The first group is important for your protection. For example, in California building codes require a degree of earthquake protection, and throughout the country, there are rules about electrical wiring. To a large extent, this first group of building codes is self-explanatory: as you go through the chapters in this book, checking each item in turn, you will learn to spot most (though not all) potentially dangerous departures from the building codes.

The second group of building codes is harder to understand, because they are sometimes a bit arbitrary. For example, why is a corridor that is (say) 42 inches wide okay, while another that is 41 inches wide considered to be in violation of code? The same is true of ceilings: why is 80 inches all right in some rooms or jurisdictions, while others require 90 inches or 100 inches?

The answer is that the same argument could be advanced progressively: if 41 inches is OK, what about 40 inches? 36 inches? 30 inches? Two feet? And while a seven foot, six inch ceiling is fine, and a seven foot (84-inch ceiling) might be tolerable, a six foot eight inch ceiling (80) inches is the least that most people could stand without feeling claustrophobic; and a six-foot ceiling would be cutting it altogether too close. These requirements are effectively limits on cost-cutting and profiteering, and there are going to be occasions when the odd inch here or there seems to be the most petty-minded bureaucracy. Well, so it is; but how else do you draw the line?

There is also a small, third group of building code requirements which seem to be the result of private jokes in the planning department, or competitions to see who can devise the meanest, most penny-pinching and trivial restriction which costs the maximum possible amount to implement. Others read like leftovers from a past age, which in many cases they are: one of the very best is not an American building regulation at all, but a regulation which says that the door of a London taxi must be big enough to admit a bale of hay for a horse. When you think about it, though, that isn't a bad way of defining door size: if you can get a bale of hay through it, *you* should be able to get in and out of the taxi reasonably comfortably.

There is not much that you can do about this third group; but in any case, they are unlikely to have much effect on private dwellings, as they were mostly devised to stop overcrowding of slum tenements.

1.6   LOOKING, CHECKING, NEGOTIATING

If there is one piece of advice that is more important than any other, it is that **there is no need to be in a hurry.** Certainly, there is always a risk that you will miss a bargain. But there is also a very significant risk that if you do *not* take your time, you will end up with a lemon. More than two thousand years ago, the Romans had a proverb: "Festina lente." Roughly translated, it is our own "Haste makes waste."

By "making haste slowly," you *greatly* increase your chances of ending up with exactly the place that you want: make no mistake, there are plenty of good places out there, so if you miss one, the chances are that you will soon find another. The way to "make haste slowly" is to do it step by step.

Looking

Begin your search slowly. Look at the real estate advertisements, talk to a couple of agents. This will help you to build up an image of what is available, what you want, and what you can realistically afford. Don't let a real estate agent get you overly excited about house-hunting — that is their job, and usually they are working for the seller — you don't want to be lured into rushing all over town, looking at houses they say are "just perfect for you!" Re-read this chapter: ask yourself what you want, and where you want it. Ask sellers and agents about expenses.

Check where the town is expanding, which neighborhoods are on the way up and which ones are on the way down. Are there are new roads planned? If so, will they pass near enough to boost the value of your property, or will they be so close that they will bring the value down? Worse still, might the place you want be in the middle of the proposed development? The city planning department can tell you a lot about this.

Don't feel too bad about "wasting other people's time." Tell them you're just looking, but that when you find the right place, you'll buy. Don't get their hopes up falsely by telling them that you'll make an offer when you have absolutely no intention of doing so.

Checking

Using your own preferences and (most importantly) the advice in this book, check out the places that look good. If they are structurally sound, and if there are no problems such as redevelopment in the area, you can afford to proceed. But if the seller or his agent is constantly pestering and badgering you, *back off*. Obviously they want to strike a deal; that's why they're selling the house. There is a difference, though, between expecting things to happen at a reasonable speed, and urging the buyer (you) to take shortcuts. Usually, the only people who benefit from shortcuts are the sellers. If they are hassling you, what are they trying to hide? What are they afraid that you are going to find out?

Negotiating

Buying a house is always easiest if you are dealing with a "motivated" seller. A motivated seller is one who *wants* to sell. It might seem that this was the only reason why anyone would put their house on the market, but as anyone who has ever bought a house can tell you, this is not necessarily so. Some sellers are "testing the water" to see what their house is worth, and whether they can afford to sell it and trade up to somewhere more expensive. Others, maybe retired people, feel that they *ought* to move to somewhere smaller and more convenient, but still retain a strong emotional attachment to the old house, so they don't really want to move. Yet others may be in disagreement about selling: he wants to, she doesn't, or vice versa.

Examples of "motivated" sellers, on the other hand, might include someone who has relocated across the country, with a big promotion and very generous moving terms from his employers. He has a real incentive to sell. Someone else might recently have been widowed. With her husband gone, she wants to move to be nearer her grown-up children. You would not want to take advantage of her, but equally, a swift sale at a far price is in the best interests of both parties. Yet a third person might have found just the house *he* wants, and have to sell quickly in order to finance it: borrowing large sums of money on a short-term "bridging loan" (interim financing) is expensive, so (once again) there is strong motivation. You might even run into someone who just plain hates the area and wants to move back to somewhere more (or less) familiar.

Because of the importance of motivation, always listen carefully to what the seller has to say. Wherever possible, reinforce their motivation. Even in the last case, you could say something like, "I know what you mean, but for me, it's the other way around. I've lived in the city all my life, and I'd go crazy in the country; but I can see that if the country is where you want to be, the city would not be much fun, either."

With all this in mind, you should be able to talk things over with the seller and come to a fair price. Because this *isn't* a book about financing there is much more about that in *How To Find A Bargain Home* — I have put what legal and financial information I have included in Appendix I. Right now, let's get down to the serious business of inspecting the property.

2.0 <u>OUTSIDE</u>

The first two things you see, the very first time you visit a house, will be the outside and the yard or garden. Because the yard is usually the easiest thing of all to fix up, I have dealt with it much later in the book; but the exterior condition of the house, even if you confine yourself to what is visible to the naked eye in five minutes, will enable you to make a very good judgment about the probable condition of the rest of the house. If you spend a few minutes going over the house with the owner, you can learn more than enough to decide whether it is worth checking everything out in detail.

Remember, your aim is always to eliminate the buildings which represent potential problems. Don't make excuses: be as ruthless as possible. There's one shingle missing? That might mean nothing — or the waterproof material under the shingle might be torn, and there might be water damage. Also, it might mean that other shingles were at risk, just waiting to disappear in the next strong wind. And that smear of green by the drainpipe: is it an innocent piece of moss, or has the water been escaping from the pipe and running down the wall for months, perhaps years? Might it have soaked in and done some *real* damage?

As I shall repeat at intervals throughout this book, I don't want to frighten you. There's no need to be frightened. The aim of the book, after all, is to spot as many problems or potential problems as possible, *before* you make any commitment; and the inspector will catch any problems that you don't, though if you follow the book carefully, you won't be calling in the building inspector until you are virtually certain that the building is sound and a good buy. If you are methodical, you can check each aspect of the house in turn, and you can see whether a particular flaw is trivial (as most of them are), or sufficiently serious to give you second thoughts. I must repeat two things, though. The first is *be methodical*. A checklist is useless unless you check **every** item: after all, what good would it do you to check the water, tires, oil, transmission fluid, power steering fluid and even windshield washer fluid before setting out on a journey, then run out of fuel because that was the one thing you hadn't checked? The second is that, although the list of possible faults that follows in this chapter may make it sound like every house is a potential deathtrap, I am (by the very nature of the book) concentrating only on those things that *can* go wrong.

In most houses, there are very few problems. The reason you bought this book, though, was to spot problems if they *do* exist; so I will not apologize any more for pointing out potential defects.

2.1   WALLS AND SIDINGS

Welcome to the world of definitions! The meaning of "wall" is clear enough (though there are structural walls, which hold the building up, and non-structural walls which serve merely to separate one space from another), and then there are *sheathings* (the "skin" of the wall, usually 8'x4' sheets of plywood), and *sidings*.

Siding (also known in some areas as *cladding*) is the board or other material that covers the outside of the building. Traditionally, siding was made of wood, overlapped in strips like the side of a clinker-built boat, but now there are also synthetic sidings (plastics, glass fiber and various kinds of composite shingle), metal sidings (normally aluminum, sometimes steel) and composite wood (plywood) sidings. Also, a coat of paint can cover a multitude of sins: even inferior-grade Masonite and other reconstituted wood products have been pressed into service by unscrupulous builders and "renovators."

Exterior walls may also be faced with brick or stone or stucco. If brick or stone is what you see, it is important to distinguish between structural materials (i.e. a wall of solid brick, stonemasonry or cinder block) and facing materials: even timber-frame houses with wood sheathing can be faced with brick or stone, and of course stucco can be applied over almost anything.

Brick

Brickwork should be flat, with no signs of bulges or cracks, and the mortar between the bricks (called the *pointing*) should be solid and dry.

Bulges in brickwork are major-league bad news. If the brickwork is solid, or if there is a brick facing on another solid masonry construction medium (such as cinder-block), bulges mean that the mortar has failed and that you are most likely looking at an *extremely* expensive rebuilding of the whole wall. If the brick is a veneer (or "skin" or "cladding") over a frame house, it means that the metal ties linking the brickwork to the wall have failed, and this also means major, expensive work.

Crumbling or (worse still) *wet* crumbling pointing between the bricks means, at the very least, that the brickwork will need to be repointed — a job which some people are happy enough to do themselves, but which is more generally regarded as a job for a skilled bricklayer, whose time does not come cheap. On the bright side, defective pointing can be confined to relatively small areas, so bad pointing in one place does not mean that the whole house is going to need repointing.

Ideally, you should check pointing with a knife blade — a professional building inspector would — but this makes some owners nervous, so a fingernail may be the hardest tool you can employ. In fact, a fingernail is very nearly as good as a penknife: really crumbly pointing will come away if you pick at it quite lightly. Also, do not be *too* worried if the pointing crumbles slightly, as long as it is dry and basically sound. The mortar between the stones at Rochester Castle can be scraped out, a grain or two at a time, with a fingernail — and the castle was built by the Normans in 1086, only a few years after they invaded England in 1066, so it has been standing for nine centuries!

The courses of brick should, of course, be straight (a "course" is a horizontal row of bricks), and the bonding should be neat and repetitive: "bonding" refers to the way the bricks are arranged, for example, *long face — short face — long face — short face*, or with only the long faces showing, but with each course half a brick out of step with the ones above and below. If the bricks are in uneven courses, or if there is no clear pattern, or if bricks are piled up like children's building blocks without the proper overlap between one course and the next, the wall will not be very strong.

Look for cracks anywhere and everywhere — they could indicate problems with the foundations, or with the ground setting — but especially look for cracks around doors and windows, where *lintels* (steel girders or wooden beams across the top) have deflected under load. Cracks in solid brick or masonry houses should put you off buying, while cracks in ornamental walls or brick cladding may or may

24

not indicate further problems. They will, however, put you on warning to check other features such as foundations (see next chapter) and even windows and doors.

With really old brick buildings, especially in cities where the air has been polluted for many decades with industrial gases, the bricks themselves may have deteriorated. Usually, though, the damage is confined to a few bricks.

Wood Siding

This is the most traditional form of siding: the white painted sidings of Colonial homes are an enduring image on postcards.

To begin with, the wooden clapboards should be straight: sagging boards indicate a long history of insufficient maintenance. Then, look at the boards from the side of the building, from the corners: the siding should be uniform and flat. Bulges are only a step away from sagging or dropped boards — unless the problem is even more serious, and the frame is out of true or the foundations are settling. Clapboard is neat, methodical stuff, and it should look that way.

If you see any suspect areas, check them carefully — but do not confine your inspection 502D*only* to suspect areas. Look for damage or rot, and for insect infestation. Modest amounts of damage may be acceptable if they can be replaced at an affordable price: re-siding the entire house can be prohibitively expensive. A thumbnail should make little impression on a good siding; if you can make a deep dent, you have problems.

While you are checking for damage and rot, also check paint. The paint should be hard and should adhere closely to the boards. Areas where the paint is dusty, flaky, cracked, blistered or peeling will have to be repainted as a matter of some urgency. You will also have to strip off the old paint, which is tedious, hard work if you do it yourself and can be expensive if you hire someone else to do it.

Pay particular attention to blistering, as this usually indicates that water has soaked through a pinhole in the paint, or that the siding was not prepared properly in the first place. Also look for a wrinkled "alligator" or "orange peel" effect, which shows that paint dried slowly and unevenly, usually as a result of poor surface preparation or (sometimes) as a result of painting in excessively humid conditions. This kind of finish is a harbinger of peeling, flaking or blistering in the not-too-distant future.

Redwood and Cedar Siding

Although wood is normally painted for protection, redwood and cedar are normally left unpainted. Although there are good aesthetic reasons for this — most people like the picturesque way in which the wood weathers to a silvery gray, with some black areas in the case of redwood — there are also technical reasons why the wood is difficult to paint: it contains oils and resins which mean that unless a good, oil-based primer is carefully applied, paint will not stick properly.

In harsh (cold, damp) climates, redwood and cedar sidings really need to be treated with a water-repellent preservative which soaks into the wood (*not* varnish!). Examine the joints and the places where the siding is fastened to the wall to see if there has been any deterioration so far.

The rules for checking shingle siding are much the same as for checking shingle roofing, which is covered in section 2.2.

Non-wood Shingle Sidings

The traditional low-cost shingle siding is of asphalt, and has a life of about twenty years. The first thing to check, after a brief general inspection, is the nail-heads: loose nails mean loose shingles, and loose shingles mean possible water entry. Really old shingles will crumble in your hands — a sure sign that it is time for replacement. Torn or otherwise damaged shingles need to be replaced as soon as possible, or water damage is a real possibility (if it hasn't occurred already), and remember that you can't replace just *one* shingle: because of the overlap, at least two must normally be lifted and replaced.

Many houses still have asbestos shingles, too. These should be inspected in much the same way as asphalt shingles, but if there is any damage, you will have to have the old shingles removed by a certified asbestos removal company, and you will find it difficult (if not impossible) to replace them with identical shingles. Asbestos shingles are often painted (and often, the paint does not adhere too well), so always *ask* what shingles are made of. Speedy re-painting of badly-painted asbestos shingles is advisable, both to seal the shingle and to prevent the release of asbestos fibers.

Vinyl Siding

Vinyl siding is usually "self colored" rather than painted (the color goes all through the material), but it seems more than usually susceptible to fading. In very cold weather, even a slight blow — a kick, a child cannoning into it, a "clip" with an automobile bumper — can crack vinyl siding. If there are cracks, or if there are any dents (less usual than with aluminum, below, but still possible), the only remedy is to remove the afflicted part and replace it. If the vinyl is more than a year or two old, replacing only part of it may give you headaches when it comes to color matching.

Try to "rattle" the siding gently to make sure that it is well secured — at the very least, loose siding needs to be nailed back in place, while it may indicate that the wall behind the siding is damaged — and (as with any other siding) make sure that it is level. Out-of-true sidings may indicate serious problems, either with the wall underneath or with settling of the foundations, or they may simply be incompetently installed, which is not too good, either.

Aluminum Siding

Aluminum siding is more durable than vinyl, and can be repainted — indeed, it must be repainted at intervals, or it will corrode. Run your hand along sections of siding to check the condition of the paint: new siding may sometimes leave a chalky deposit on your hand (if it's that new, the owner should still have the warranty somewhere), but normally this is a sign that it's time to repaint. More modern sidings will usually have vent holes at the bottom; older sidings will not.

Light alloy will not shatter like vinyl, but it will dent easily, and dented areas cannot be economically repaired: they must be replaced. Because aluminum conducts electricity very well, you should also check to see that the siding is grounded, preferably in more than one place. Otherwise, check aluminum siding in much the same way as vinyl siding.

Steel Siding

Steel siding is stronger than either vinyl or light alloy, but it is also heavier and it will rust unless it is protected with a good paint. Otherwise, check as for aluminum siding, including checking electrical grounding.

Siding and Insulation

Insulation is more appropriately dealt with in Chapter 4, "Systems and Services," but it is worth noting here that metal or vinyl siding may be installed "as is" or over a backup or insulation board. The insulation board can make a very significant difference to the overall insulation of the house — thin metal and vinyl sidings have virtually no heat-retaining ability — and it can also make for greater strength and resistance to dents.

Stucco

Stucco is a classic "cover-up" material: indeed, the reason why the White House was originally covered with white stucco was to remove the evidence of damage caused by the British in the War of 1812! It is a mixture of Portland cement and sand, and it can be applied over almost anything — wood or stone, sound or unsound.

As normally applied to frame houses in the United States, stucco is normally trowelled onto wire mesh ("expanded metal") which is fastened to the wall sheathing with a layer of roofing paper in between as a moisture barrier.

Look for cracks, since they permit water entry and should be repaired immediately, and for bulges. When you see a bulge, tap it to see how it sounds. It may be that this is merely a thick area of stucco (the skill with which the stuff is applied varies widely), but if it sounds hollow, that is more of a problem.

Small hollow bulges usually mean either that the stucco has pulled away from the expanded metal or that the stucco and the expanded metal together have pulled away from the wall sheathing. This can be fairly expensive to fix, but it is not necessarily cause for rejecting the house out of hand.

Large hollow bulges are another matter. Normally they indicate that the foundations have settled unevenly, which is bad news, but they may also indicate that the actual frame of the house is not solid enough to support the sheathing and stucco — and that also means *real* expense.

Beware of Too-Good Exteriors

It is said that doctors bury their mistakes, and that cooks eat theirs; but builders just cover them up. If an otherwise slightly run-down house is covered with superb new siding or freshly-applied or re-coated stucco, ask yourself what the owner is trying to hide.

Replacing Siding

Despite the claims of "do-it-yourself" magazines, it is usually cheaper in the long run (and it is almost always easier and less time consuming) to have the work done by a professional contractor. The additional cost will be offset by two factors: the discount which the contractor gets on the siding (you would probably pay more for the same siding if you wanted to install it yourself), and the very much greater speed and lesser disruption with which the contractor can do the job. In other words, ageing siding over a basically sound structure is easily replaced — but if it needs to be replaced, make sure that this is reflected in the price that you pay for the house.

2.2   ROOFING

Where I was born, in Cornwall, some of the older houses are still part "cob." "Cob" is the local name for adobe, rammed earth, or (as we say in English) mud. But there is a saying that "with a good hat, and a good pair of boots, cob will last forever." The "good pair of boots" is a stone foundation; the "good hat" is a good roof. The old saying is right, too: some of those adobe walls are hundreds of years old.

Certainly, a good roof is one of the most important things to look for when you are inspecting a house: as long as the roof is sound and waterproof, you can do as much renovation as you like inside. But if the roof leaks, fixing it must be your *very highest* priority, or water damage will set at nought all your attempts to improve the interior.

Once again, don't be unnecessarily frightened by roofing "problems." Unless the roof has been neglected for some time, there is unlikely to be any serious damage as a result of water entry: your only real expense, if you decide to buy the house, will lie in repairing the immediate problem with the roof. Of course, if the roof *does* have problems, you will be put on your guard to look for any damage that might have resulted.

Regardless of the roofing material, take note of the *pitch* or steepness of the roof, and of the presence or absence of parapets (low walls surrounding the roof). Steep pitches shed snow and water faster, but are essential only in areas where snow is heavy or where torrential rain is commonplace. Even a flat roof can withstand downpours if they occur only one or two months a year (though the roof should slope very slightly, so that water drains and does not lie in puddles), but snow is another matter: a square foot of snow, twelves inches deep, is likely to weigh anything from five to ten pounds. On a 1000-square foot roof, that's 5,000 to 10,000 pounds, or anything up to about five tons.

Parapets may add a certain elegance to a building, but they are much inferior to overhanging eaves. Even without snow, they can trap all manner of unsavory detritus (dead birds, old nests, leaves, wind-blown paper and more), and in an area prone to snow, they are a disaster. Also, they provide an additional "valley" where water can collect, which means that they have to be sealed, traditionally with "flashing" (defined in a later paragraph).

A pair of binoculars, or even a telescope, is all but essential for the preliminary roof inspection, which you can do from the street.

30

("Typical Roof Framing and Construction" Illustration)

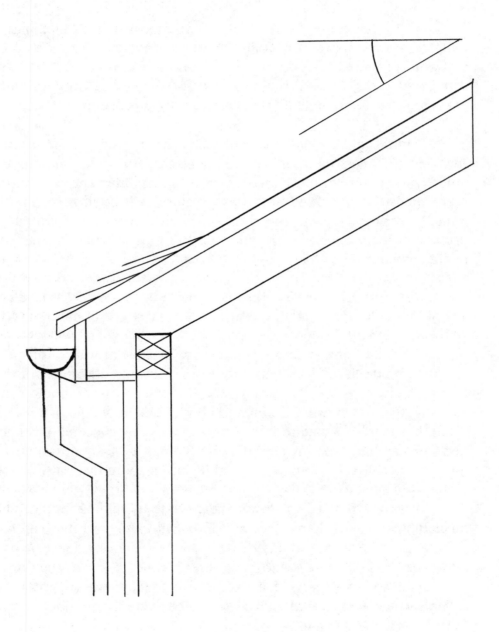

Figure A

Slate

A good slate roof is massively heavy, and very expensive to replace (though it can be restored and re-felted, under the slate, at a much more reasonable price). It also lasts a very, very long time: the best slate roofs are 250 years old or more, and 50-100 years is the minimum you should expect before the slates need to be re-hung. Even the most inferior slates should last 30-50 years. The only things that can harm slate roofs are *very* high winds (over, say, 60 mph) and *very* large hailstones (larger than pigeon's eggs).

The only thing you can easily check from the street is whether there are any missing slates, which are easily replaced, and as usual, any missing weatherproofing should lead you to inspect the area underneath for rain damage. If any of the slates is skewed or out of place, you should also suspect the condition of the nails (see below).

When you get inside the house, you will need to check the condition of the roof timbers (though a sagging ridge-beam will be evident from outside), but that is not something you can do now. If you can inspect the outside of the roof, though, check the condition of the nails on which the slates are hung; they can, after many decades, rust through.

Tile

Terra cotta tile is not quite as durable as the finest slate — or to be accurate, it tends to require more maintenance — but it is still capable of outlasting the building it protects: in some cities, there is quite a business of recycling 50- and 100-year-old tiles from houses that are being demolished. Otherwise, look out for much the same things with tile as you would with slate.

Wood Shingles

Good-quality wood shingles can be surprisingly durable, with a forty-year life by no means unusual. For your own peace of mind (and by law in some areas), wooden shingles must, however, be treated with some kind of fire-retarding process. Look for the same sort of problems as with slate and tile, but remember that the roof can be very much more lightly built than it would need to be for tile or (especially) for slate.

Synthetic Shingles

Synthetic (asphalt-based) shingles may not be beautiful, and they rarely last more than about 25 years, but they are cheap, which is why they are widely used.

The big thing to watch out for with asphalt-shingled roofs (apart from the usual cautions about missing or damaged shingles) is double-layering or (worse still) triple-layering. While you can lay an extra layer of shingles over the first layer, it is *not* good practice to lay a third layer on top of that. Rather, the existing layers must be stripped off and you have to begin again. This is obviously much more expensive than re-roofing over the old shingles, but if you don't do it properly, you run the risk of water creeping between the three (or more) layers of shingles and getting into the roof and causing damage.

If the present owner does not know how old the roof is or how many layers there are, you can generally spot multiple-layer roofing by standing about ten yards from the building and trying to see if the shingles lie flat on the roof. If there is any sign of waviness or "cupping," it means there are two or more layers: singles expand and contract differently as they get older, and it is this differential expansion and contraction that causes the waviness.

Asphalt Paper

Most flat roofs are covered with asphalt paper, which is effectively a sort of giant shingle applied from a roll. It is an excellent material, because it has very few joins, but it does have one very significant drawback: it rarely lasts much more than a decade. This means that re-roofing is a regular (though not particularly expensive) undertaking.

Look for blisters, which generally indicate ageing, though if the roof looks new and the owner assures you that it was recovered recently, a blister may simply mean that a lazy roofer failed to "pop" an

("Typical Flat Roof Construction" Illustration)

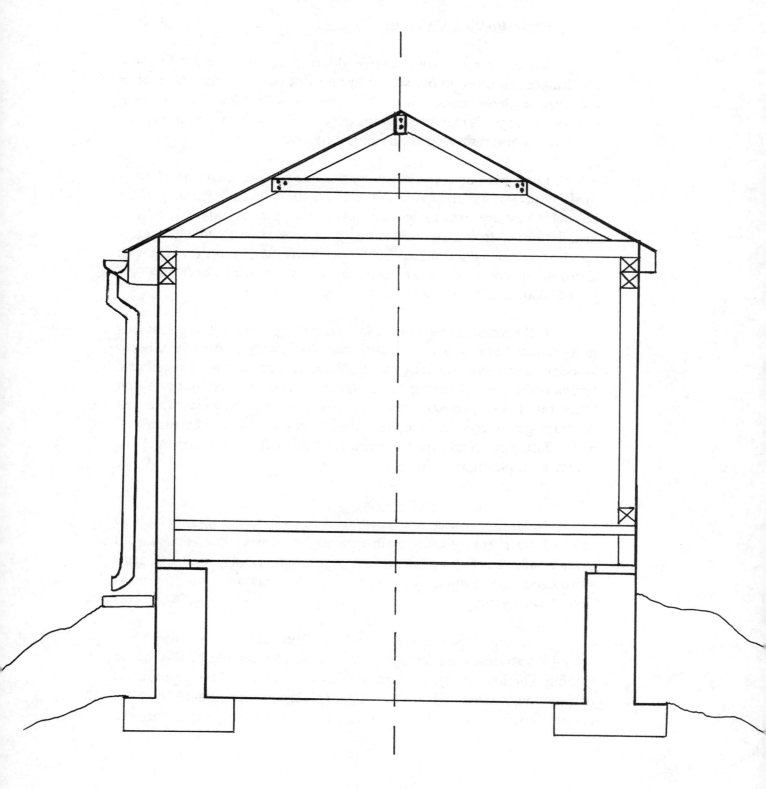

Figure B

old blister before laying the new material. Generally, an older asphalt-paper roof has a worn, eroded look anyway.

Other Roofing Materials

Some flat roofs are covered with cement, which is far from an ideal material; often, there will be a network of lines where cracks in the cement have been "tarred" or sealed with bitumen. Rarely, bitumen or asphalt may be used to cover the whole roof: this absorbs a tremendous amount of heat on sunny days.

Lead, zinc or copper may be used as roofing materials in their own right, though they are normally used only for "flashing" (see below). They are extremely expensive, both in materials cost and in installation: a friend of mine had to restore something between a hundred and two hundred square feet of lead (used in conjunction with slate) on the roof of his Victorian house, and the *materials* cost was over $3000!

Galvanized corrugated iron is not as popular a roofing material in the United States as it is in some countries, notably Australia, but it is found. The drawbacks are poor insulation, condensation problems, and noise (hail on a corrugated iron roof can sound like machine-gun fire!), but it is surprisingly cheap initially. In the unlikely even that you are buying a place with a corrugated-iron roof, pay particular attention to the fastening of the roof to the structure of the building: rust here will make replacement difficult.

Flashing and Tarring

I have mentioned "flashing" several times now. Flashing is traditionally lead (or sometimes zinc and, rarely, copper), but galvanized iron flashing is now used quite widely and you may even find plastic flashing.

Basically, flashing is a curved piece of waterproofing that seals the joint between a vertical wall and a roof, whether the roof is flat or sloping. The lower edge rests on the roof (whether asphalt paper, slate or anything else), while the upper edge is protected by the counterflashing, which is set into the wall, or by some other form of overhang or protective coat. The idea is never to have an open, unprotected edge which is either horizontal or upward-facing: all open or potentially open edges must be downward-facing so that they shed water.

Flashing is needed when any vertical wall breaks the line of the roof, so flashing is found around parapet walls, chimneys, inspection covers, and skylights. Always check the condition of both flashing and counterflashing: it is quite expensive to have it replaced, but it is madness to buy a house with defective flashing and not to attend to it *immediately*, as it is a fruitful source of water entry and potentially of severe damage.

Sometimes, instead of flashing, tar or bitumen is used. ***This is only a short-term solution***. Sooner or later the tar or bitumen will shrink and pull away from the gap which it was supposed to be protecting. Sure, you could have the same job done again ... and again ... and again, but it's better to pay to have the job done properly, so that you will not have to think about the matter again for decades.

Coping

A coping is a course of stones or tiles that is laid along the top of an exposed wall (such as a parapet) in order to protect the top of the wall from water which might otherwise seep in. Cracked or missing copings, or loose mortar, can once again let in one of the most dreaded of homeowners' enemies: water. If there is no serious existing damage as a result of the defective coping, though, this is not an expensive problem to solve.

2.3   GUTTERS AND DRAINPIPES

Some houses just do not have any gutters: the rain or snow slides straight off the roof. While this is admirably simple, and suitable for climates in the Sun Belt where it rarely rains, it also means that anyone who is walking under the eaves is going to be subjected to a steady stream of water when it is raining!

Also, in areas where rain is frequent, it is a good idea to lead the water away from the house. Otherwise, it can collect in puddles all around the house and even lead to seepage into the basement or uneven settling of the foundations. This is one of the main reasons why drainpipes or "leaders" are so important.

At one time, gutters used to be made of copper or galvanized iron, though today you are more likely to find either aluminum or plastic, both of which are more resistant to corrosion than galvanized iron and much cheaper than copper. Galvanized iron gutters (and drainpipes) are likely to be badly corroded, because they were a cheap option when they were installed and they needed to be painted regularly to protect them, and even copper gutters should be considered as candidates for automatic replacement. If you can see that some of the old guttering has already been replaced, you can bet that the rest is likely to need replacing, too.

Gutters and Fasteners

Check (by eye or with a spirit level if you get the chance) that the gutters actually slope in the right direction: some don't, especially if they were installed by home handymen, so that the water pours out about halfway along, or near the end that was supposed to have ben sealed, instead of flowing into the downspout. A gutter which is blocked by leaves or other debris can, of course, have much the same problem. this is not only inconvenient; it can also lead, in the long term, to water damage to the fascia board that carries the gutters. If the gutters look as if they have not been cleaned for a long time (you'll need a ladder to check this), look extra hard at the woodwork beside the gutters for signs of water damage.

Check the condition of the gutter fasteners, too. For some reason, loose gutters seem to hold a terrible fascination for the hammer-and-nails school of do-it-yourself home maintenance men, and instead of replacing the fasteners or brackets, they will try a four-inch nail as a cure-all. Ugly or broken gutters are one of those things which make a house look run-down and are a good negotiating point, but they are not particularly expensive or difficult to fix.

Drainpipes

Obviously, check that the drainpipe is connected to the gutters; it is surprising how often they are not, because a section of guttering is missing.

Some drainpipes simply follow the wall down, then stop about a foot above the ground and discharge the water onto the ground. This is not a good idea, because it concentrates the water in one place and greatly increases the risk of damage to the foundations or of seepage into the basement. Also, it means that the section of wall beneath the opening is constantly scoured by water under pressure, which again creates a risk of water damage.

At the very least, there should be a right-angled bend in the drain which directs the water outward and away from the house, and it is better if this bend is either continued for a short distance or is directed into a drain or concrete gully, once again reducing the risk of water damage.

In many houses, the drainpipe empties into an existing drain, which might seem ideal but can bring problems of its own. Over the years, leaves, bird nests and other detritus can collect in the drainpipe, blocking it at the bottom and leading to a hidden backing-up of water which can percolate into the foundations. A small wire-mesh cap or dome over the top of the drainpipe will do a great deal to relieve this problem, but the only real solution is to clean the drainpipe occasionally; once a year is plenty often enough.

To see if the drain has been blocked in the past, look for dampness or moss or mold around the base of the pipe, and look at the back of the pipe (which is where the seam will be) to see if it has been split. A split typically indicates frost damage, showing that water was standing in the pipe and then froze. Also, when you get inside the house, look for signs of seepage (dampness or mold again) near the base of the drain pipe.

2.4   WINDOWS AND DOORS

There is more to windows and doors than immediately meets the eye. A window must not only admit light (and air, if it opens), it must also be secure and well insulated. I shall come back to window insulation, but unless a window *fits* properly, it will be a source of drafts and rattles.

Wooden Windows

The two most traditional types of wooden windows are vertically-sliding double-hung sash windows, with a counterweight and conventionally opening casement windows. In harsh climates double-hung sash windows can be a source of drafts and rattles, and if the sash cords break, they are messy and time-consuming to repair (you have to pull the window to pieces). Unless you particularly like the look, therefore, or unless the alternatives would be architectural vandalism, you who live in extreme climates may want to consider replacing them even if there is nothing much wrong.

Among the things that can go wrong are broken sash-cords, rotted frames, jambs or (quite often) rotted sills, ageing putty (which needs to be knifed out and replaced), lack of paint (quite common if the original windows are protected with outer storm windows), and an excess of paint, so that the windows are "painted shut" and you will need to get in there with a penknife before you can even open them to strip off the old paint and apply new.

Much the same problems can be encountered with conventionally-opening casement windows — the ones that open and close like doors — with the additional problem that the frames sometimes warp or well so that the window cannot be closed properly without some sanding or planing.

In all fairness, though, I have lived or stayed in houses where the wooden window frames are 75 years old or more, but where good initial quality and careful maintenance — mostly, regular painting *after* stripping off the old paint — mean that the windows are still as good as the day they were installed. Old wooden frames are never going to be as energy-efficient as double-glazed alloy or vinyl windows with a thermal break, but they do look good and they are very "homey." You have to make a trade-off between tradition and modern advantages.

You can also buy modern wooden double-glazed window units, ready-built. These are just as energy efficient as properly-made metal or vinyl-coated windows, as well as being rather more attractive. They require maintenance — painting or varnishing — just like the older windows, but they arguably have the advantages of both the old and the new. They are, however, a little more expensive than any but the best metal windows.

Metal and Vinyl Windows

Most modern windows are made of light alloy, often with a vinyl coating; some are of wood with a vinyl coating. There is not much to check on these, except for the quality of the double glazing and the presence of a thermal break, as described in the next section. They should, of course, fit well, and this cannot be taken for granted. Also check the quality of the joins at the corners.

Even if metal or vinyl-coating windows were not installed when the house was built, they are obtainable in designs which can be slotted straight into an old double-hung sash window, after the sash and counterweights have been removed. Alternatively (though they are less usual) you may be able to find modern windows in double-hung sash style, though these will cost more than straight drop-in, non-opening windows.

If modern windows have not been installed already, you may wish to consider doing this. Check prices, using the Yellow Pages: it can be a useful bargaining point to say, "Of course, all these windows will have to be replaced, and that will cost $1200" (or whatever figure you have come up with).

One thing that you do *not* want, if you can help it, is the old style of metal-framed, single-glazed windows. These things are unbelievably poor insulators, and in winter they will put your heating bill up spectacularly unless they are covered with heavy curtains. They are also magnets for condensation, which you will often see running down the glass.

Double-Glazing and Window Coatings

Double-glazing is exactly what its name suggests: each window consists of two panes of glass, some distance apart. This results in a very much higher degree of thermal insulation, and a surprising amount of extra sound insulation, too, but there are several things you should know about the different types of windows.

Separation — The best distance between the two panes in a double-glazed unit is apparently still a matter of scientific dispute: some favor a smaller gap, and others a larger gap. It seems that, at the moment, neither wide gaps (typically up to four inches) nor narrow gaps (as little as 1/8") can be regarded as clearly superior; and there is next to nothing to choose between (say) a quarter-inch gap and a half-inch gap.

Thermal Break — One thing that *is* very important, though, is the use of an insulating material between the edges of the glass. Many early double-glazed windows were solid aluminum, which is an excellent conductor of heat and therefore a very poor insulator. A "thermal break" consists of a much poorer conductor of heat between the inner metal panel and the outer metal panel. this may be of wood or of vinyl, but it will greatly increase the insulating quality of the windows and reduce condensation.

Gas Fillings — Early double-glazed windows were often just air-spaced, and some were even *deliberately* made with "breather" holes to avoid condensation between the panels. More modern windows are normally carefully sealed, and may be filled with a variety of gases: dry air, nitrogen, or even argon. I have heard of windows which are built on the same principle as a vacuum flask, with *no* gas between the two panes, but I have never actually seen them. Like the size of the gap, there is very little practical scientific evidence on what is best.

If you can see condensation *inside* the windows, you can do one of three things. You can replace the unit; you can learn to live with it (the loss in insulating efficiency is usually negligible); or you may be able to disassemble the window (or have it disassembled) and fit a new seal.

Triple-Glazing — The additional benefits of triple-glazing (three sheets of glass instead of one) are, to say the least, questionable. Triple-glazing is bulkier, *much* more expensive, and can be obtrusive: all that glass gives the view through the window a greenish tinge and creates an effect somewhat akin to living in an aquarium. *Good* double glazing should be more than sufficient for all but the most severe climates.

Coatings — "Low-E" coatings, applied to the glass in the windows, reflect heat away from the exterior in the summer, and back into the interior in the winter. They are very valuable *if* you live in a harsh climate and *if* you have large areas of windows (especially picture windows), and *if* the house is not really designed for the climate, for example, if there are no overhanging eaves to shade the windows in warm weather. There is no doubt that these coatings work, but there is equally little doubt that in many domestic applications their effect is not very great. Certainly, they are not worth paying a fortune for.

"R" and "U" Values — Manufacturer's catalogs for windows will often quote "R" values (thermal resistance values) and "U" values (heat transfer coefficients). Although these look very scientific, their real-world value is limited, and the insulating quality of an individual window is a fairly small part of the overall energy efficiency of a house. Only if the rest of the house is very well insulated, with no gaps under any doors and no rattling windows, do variations in "R" and "U" values begin to have any particular impact.

Does this Affect You, Anyway? — If you live in a place where winters are never very cold, most of this insulation information is, in any case, of marginal interest. In a winter in upstate New York, where my wife comes from, maintaining a 70° temperature indoors would regularly mean temperature differentials of up to 80° or 90° between the interior and the exterior, sometimes more, and often in conditions of howling wind and snow.

Even in a desert state like Arizona, on the other hand, keeping the temperature down to 85° in 105° heat means a 20° temperature differential, and most people could tolerate a higher setting on the air conditioner than that. Winds are modest or negligible, and there's certainly no snow to worry about in that temperature! What I am saying is that it is possible to worry too much about energy efficient insulation, when cutting out a single unnecessary car trip each month would have more impact on the environment and your pocket book.

Doors and Door Glazing

Exterior doors are normally of three kinds: unglazed (solid wood), partially glazed (with some glass), or fully glazed (mostly glass). They may be of wood, or some fully-glazed doors may use light alloy or even steel.

Obviously, the door should fit snugly in order to avoid drafts and rattles. Check the space all around the door, especially underneath. If it is a wooden door, check for any sign of rot or deterioration, especially around the bottom. Also check the frame and hinges (a good new door can be installed in a half-rotten frame), and the area around the lock, which should be sound. Consider security as well as comfort issues. It is frightening how easily some doors can be opened with a smart karate-style kick to the area of the lock, which splinters the frame.

The same comments about energy efficiency apply to glazed doors as apply to windows: double glazing, with a thermal break and preferably a dry inert atmosphere between the panes, is the least you should look for. Doors with single-skin glass will lose a *lot* of heat in cold weather.

An unglazed door is almost invariably more secure than a glazed door, except possibly in the case of armored glass. On the other hand, different types of glazed doors (including French windows) vary widely in security.

The least secure type of all is often the sliding door: some designs can simply be lifted off their runners, even from outside the house. Always check sliding doors to see if this is possible. If it is, you may be able to jam the door very effectively with a piece of wood or with a screw that stops the doors being opened; or you may not be able to do anything. This is something you have to work out for yourself.

Next in the range of security comes the door with small panes of glass (usually in a relatively small area at the top), and *only* a "Yale" type lock without a deadbolt or any other form of security. A would-be villain can smash a single pane of glass, then reach in and open the door. I once had to do this myself when I had locked myself out! On the other hand, if you add a good "Bramah" or "Chubb" type lock, the sort that must be locked with a key, this sort of door is as secure as a solid wood door, provided (a) that the door is in fact locked with the deadbolt, which mine obviously wasn't when I locked myself out, and (b) that the glass area is too small to permit easy entry even if all the glass is kicked out.

The third type of door which can make life very easy for the burglar is one with large panels of thin glass, or with smaller panels separate only by thin wood (half-inch or three-quarter-inch). A smart kick with a heavy boot can smash straight through one of these doors; a would-be burglar has only to wrap himself in a thick blanket or an old coat and walk straight through.

Modern doors, with alloy frames and large areas of toughened glass (preferably double-glazed) are actually harder to break than the old multi-panel type. Even so, it is better to have the door which has two large panels (or four or more smaller ones), separated by light-alloy strips, and secured with a Bramah-type lock; it is possible (though difficult) to kick out the whole of a single, large panel, leaving a hole which is very little more obstruction than an open door.

Storm Doors

The ideal state of affairs, both from the point of insulation and from the standpoint of security, is to have a double set of doors: a strong, outer set of unglazed storm doors with a deadbolt, which you close when you want maximum insulation and security, and an inner glazed door which is lighter and more welcoming. If this is not already installed, consider how easily it might be done. Many insurance companies will give you a discount on your insurance if you have this sort of arrangement.

2.5 LOCKS AND SECURITY

Security systems, in the sense of burglar alarms, intruder detectors and the like, are covered in Section 4.5: here, we are concerned with old-fashioned security in the shape of stout doors and strong locks. There is an old saying, "Locks only keep out honest people," and while it is true that a sufficiently determined burglar can gain admission almost anywhere, it is also true that most criminals are basically lazy and will look for the easiest targets. If your house is too hard to get into, they will usually go somewhere else.

Window Locks

Most types of windows can be effectively locked, but the types of locks for the different windows vary widely. There is little point in describing them in detail, because if they are fitted you will be able to judge their efficacy, and if they are not fitted you will be well advised to go to a good hardware store and see what they have.

It is worth saying, though, that there is a major difference between those locks which can easily be operated from the inside, and those which cannot. The ones that can be operated from the inside are convenient for the homeowner, but they are also convenient for the thief, if he has managed to gain entrance some other way — for instance, by smashing a window. the ones that require some sort of key are less convenient for the owner and very much less convenient for the thief.

Door Locks

Once again, the only thing that is worth saying is that *as a rule*, "Yale" type locks (the ones that use keys like large automobile keys) are rather less secure than "Bramah" or "Chubb" type deadbolt locks which use the bigger, old-fashioned keys. There are, however, good "Yale" type locks and bad "Bramah" or "Chubb" type locks (all these names are trademarks, and they all make excellent locks). I just would not want to live in a house that only had a standard, builder-installed cheap copy of a "Yale" lock; I'd want to add something else.

You may also want to consider changing the locks if you buy the house, though in most decent neighborhoods with decent sellers (and you can tell, usually), you may decide not to bother. On the other hand, I know one couple in a very pleasant area whose house was burled by a relative who was hooked on drugs and who (before he developed the habit) was given a set of keys. I feel sorry for anyone who buys that house and does not have the locks changed.

I also like to have bolts on my exterior doors, preferably at both top and bottom: a bolted door is easy to open from the inside, but offers immense resistance to any kind of attempt to kick it in from the outside. Whether you use a security chain or not, or a "Judas window" sort of viewer installed in the door, is up to you. "Judas windows" are very easy and cheap to install in timber doors (you just drill a hole about half an inch or less in diameter), and they allow you to check who is out there before you even consider opening the door.

Grilles and Shutters

Years ago, many houses had big, heavy wooden shutters that closed *inside* the windows. These had numerous advantages: they were light-tight, they were excellent insulators, and they were very secure. They were also heavy, cumbersome and expensive, so they became less and less common.

If the house you are looking at is in an area of town that has had more than its fair share of burglaries, though, you should consider your shutter options: if shutters are already fitted (including the European roller-shutter type that is so popular in Mediterranean countries), this can be a big plus.

Grilles are another possibility: they are increasingly popular in Southern California, where they are usually of wrought-iron Spanish design, rather than "prison-window" bars. They are available both for windows and doors. Although they are excellent for security, there is an important question you should ask yourself: how easy would it be for you to get *out*, in the event of an emergency, such as a fire?

Perhaps even more importantly, how easily could your children get out? Unless the homeowner can demonstrate how to get out *fast*, you should think twice about the usefulness of grilles, and ask yourself how easy it would be to modify them for better safety.

3.0   INSIDE: STRUCTURE AND LAYOUT

By the time you have finished examining the points listed in Chapter Two, you should have a pretty good idea of whether or not you want to investigate the property further.

It may well be that so far, you have discovered absolutely no serious faults. Good! As I have emphasized a number of times throughout the book, you are much more likely to find a good house than you are to encounter the catalog of disasters that appears on these pages. This book, though, is aimed at helping you to *avoid* these disasters, which is why I have to discuss them all in such detail.

If you have discovered no serious faults so far, it is <u>likely</u> (though far from *certain*) that the building is structurally sound. Checking the structure, though, is no more difficult than checking all the features that were described in the last chapter, and it will add immeasurably to your peace of mind.

Of course, if you have discovered minor faults on the outside — a missing shingle or two, or a drain spout which simply stops a foot or so above the ground and discharges close to the foundations of the house — then you will have been put on your guard to make further checks, usually for water damage, when you get inside.

While you are checking the structural integrity of the house, you will also be checking the layout and "livability." If there are unconventional features, such as a single downstairs bathroom in a two-story house where all the bedrooms are upstairs, ask yourself if you can <u>really</u> live with this. Likewise, if you have to go through one of the so-called bedrooms in order to get to the bathroom, ask yourself if you can really count this as a bedroom at all. It might (or might not) be suitable for a small child, but if you have guests or even if your children are more than five or six, it is unlikely to be a genuinely usable bedroom. The technical term, incidentally, is an "obligated" room. Unusual layouts of this type are normally found only in older houses, but they are worth looking out for.

The only danger at this point is that if the external inspection has been favorable, you may already have started to "fall in love" with the place. Just like falling in love with a person, falling in love with a house can blind you to faults which would be obvious to anyone else. Either you simply don't see them, or you see them, but decide that they are minor or unimportant. Now is the time to be on your guard, because structural repairs can get you into **serious** expense.

Your most useful tools for inspecting the structure of a building are a small, powerful flashlight; a set of overalls, if you want to get into crawl spaces and attics; and possibly a spirit level, which is much easier than judging things by eye. A tiny one, no more than four inches long, is easy to carry and can tell you a surprising amount. Incidentally, you may wish to consider one of the new generation of flashlights with the Xenon bulbs: I use a Maglite Mini-Mag, which is pocket size (it uses only two AA batteries) but is much more powerful than you might think believable, and which can be focused from a broad "flood" light to a tight "spot" beam.

If you are looking at really old properties, you may also wish to carry a plumb line. We are so accustomed to walls that really are upright and right angles that really are right angles, that we sometimes find it hard to believe when a wall is out of true. A plumb line can help you believe the evidence of your own eyes: no, that wall *really does* slope slightly to the left.

3.1   <u>FOUNDATIONS</u>

The foundations are ... well ... the foundation of a sound house. Unless the foundations are solid, you have the potential for disaster. In the words of the Gospel According to St. Matthew:

> *Every one that heareth these sayings of mine*
> *and doeth them not, shall be likened unto a foolish*
> *man, which built his house upon the sand:*

> *And the rain descended, and the floods*
> *came, and the winds blew, and beat upon that*
> *house; and it fell; and great was the fall of it.*

Modern foundations in the United Sates are almost always of poured concrete, which is arguably the best variety. In states with stringent earthquake regulations, notably California, the foundations ares so solid that they constitute a "raft" on which the house is built; and even if the ground moves, the structural integrity of the "raft" (more usually called a "pad") should not be affected.

Sometimes, instead of being poured, foundations are "built" in the same way as a wall and of the same materials: concrete blocks, brick, or even stone. Some buildings are even built on compacted rubble. This sounds terrible, but it is a perfectly good way of doing things: in Europe, there are buildings which have been standing for many hundreds of years on a rubble foundation. A great deal depends on the solidity of the underlying soil, and on the site, as described earlier in Section 1.2.

It is also quite possible that two (or more) types of foundations are to be found in the same house, especially if it has been extended or rebuilt. You should read all of the sections on foundations below, because although some faults (such as efflorescence) are more common in one sort of foundation wall than another, most faults can appear in almost any kind of foundation.

Regardless of the type of foundation, you are looking for two things: cracks and moisture damage. While neither of these would be grounds for rejecting a house out of hand, you need to be *very* sure that the damage is (a) repairable at a reasonable cost and (b) unlikely to recur.

Poured Concrete

Not only is poured concrete one of the best types of foundation: it is also one of the easiest to check. Cracks are readily visible because (by definition) the concrete should be flat and flawless.

Even so, small cracks *are* sometimes found, and if they are, you *must* get a report from a building inspector or structural engineer before you buy the house. Even if they are not threat to the structure of the house, there is always the ever-present threat that unless they are repaired, you run the risk of water entry and ever-increasing repair bills.

In fact, even large cracks are not necessarily cause for rejecting a house, but if you find them, you must satisfy yourself on the following points:

50

Large unrepaired cracks are so serious that they are grounds for rejecting any house unless the price of the house is greatly reduced *and* you can get a binding estimate from a contractor to repair them.

Large *un*repaired cracks may or may not be serious. Ask the home owner when the crack was repaired and what sort of guarantee came with the repair. Typically, it is for five years. If the repair is recent (in the last year or two) and there is no further sign of cracking, you may decide that the crack is a risk you can live with. If the repair is very old (twenty years or more in the past), and again there is no further sign of cracking, you may decide that the house has probably settled all that it is going to settle, so once again, the risk is not great.

If there is any sign of further cracking, regardless of the age of the house or of the repair, you would need to have *very good* reasons before deciding that you were not going to reject the building. Also, even if there are no immediate signs of damage or further cracking, you would do well to beware of a repair that was between five and ten years old: old enough to be out of warranty, but not really old enough to demonstrate that the same thing would not happen again.

This, incidentally, is one of the strongest arguments for hiring a good, local building inspector who has lived in the area for many years. He may be able to say something like, "Oh yes, that damage dates to the very wet winter of '81 (or whenever). Half the houses in the area will have something like that — I wouldn't worry about it too much." Or, of course, he may say, "most of the buildings around here are built thus and so, because of the flooding (or earthquakes, or mudslides, or whatever), and the foundations on this one are not as well made as they should be." Of course, you can find out a certain amount of this for yourself just by talking to people (assuming that you are not a long-time resident yourself), but the building inspector obviously has the "inside track" as a result of his specialist experience.

Concrete Block

Concrete block foundation walls should be inspected in much the same way as poured concrete, but with the proviso that cracks can be harder to spot. In particular, look closely at the corners: I have even seen corners that have separated in a unit, though this is obviously an extreme case. If the corner has "fallen off," then an intolerable strain is likely to be imposed on the structure of the house, and if the walls have not already sagged in places, it is only a matter of time.

Concrete block foundations are also more liable than poured concrete walls to bulging. An inward bulge in a foundation wall indicates pressure from the outside and one of the most usual causes of pressure is waterlogged earth. In a "worst-case" scenario, the foundation wall could even burst like a dam, "and great will be the fall thereof."

If you have already spotted a warning sign, such as a drainpipe which discharges directly onto the ground beside the foundation wall, this could explain the waterlogging — or there might be a spring, or an old stream, which would be very much harder to deal with. Once again, this is the sort of thing where, if you did decide to hire a building inspector, you would want very specific assurances about the continuing safety of the foundations.

Brick

Brick foundation walls with their smaller "building blocks" and much greater reliance on mortar and bonding, require the highest skill in building. a well-built brick foundation is enormously strong, but a poorly built one is a weak, feeble structure that will "give" at the slightest movement of the soil. Look for massive, solid construction; sound mortar; and a regular, "bonded" structure in which the bricks are laid in a way that always places the joint between a "sandwich" of two other bricks. Watch for bulging, too.

Brick foundations are also more liable than either poured concrete or concrete blocks to efflorescence. This is a "frosty" or even "moldy" appearance which is caused by minerals being leached out of the brick: it is always white or brownish-white in color. Efflorescence clearly indicates dampness and very often means that you will need (expensive) waterproofing done if you decide to buy the house. If the efflorescence is very old, or if the walls have a damp course installed (see Glossary), this may, however, be a comparatively minor problem with brick. Efflorescence with concrete may also have occurred when the concrete was poured. Once again, if you decide that you are interested enough in the house to want to hire a building inspector, this is one of the questions you should put to him.

Efflorescence should not be confused with genuine mold or algae, which is usually seen as a green or green-brown covering on the wall and is wet, rather than merely damp, to the touch. This kind of moisture may be very serious indeed, or it may be quickly and easily curable. I was horrified when mold appeared on the interior of my brick-built house, but the cause was simple enough: a blocked drainpipe outside, so that water was running down the wall instead of through the down-spout. I had to repaper the wall, but unblocking the down-spout cured the problem immediately and the wall took less then a week to dry out.

Stone

Only very old houses are likely to have stone foundations, and anything that is going to happen to such a house should already have happened. Stone foundations are, however, the very hardest of all types of foundation to inspect because the stones are often rough and irregular: small cracks may be almost impossible to detect and even quite large ones may not be easy to spot. On the bright side, any house with stone foundations is likely to be so old that you can almost assume there are no problems with the foundation: if there were, the house itself would have settled or would show other signs of damage.

Rubble

With a rubble (landfill) foundation, a great deal depends on what is done on top of the rubble, For example, a poured concrete foundation on top of rubble is probably the finest foundation you can have; it is only expense that stops this from being a much more popular way of building foundations.

Even if the foundations are built (instead of poured) on top of the rubble, you should still have an excellent foundation. Drainage is usually first class and, provided the rubble is thick enough, the risk of ground subsidence is greatly reduced: the weight of the rubble and the way that it is compacted should mean that the ground was well settled to begin with, and the rubble can actually move and shift a little to take up further movement of the ground without necessarily affecting the foundations.

Take note, though, of the proviso "if the rubble is thick enough." A builder who was building his own home might use three <u>feet</u> or more of builders' rubble; a "cowboy" who was building houses quickly as a speculative venture might use as little as four or five <u>inches</u>. Once again, a rubble foundation is one of those things that you will want to ask the building inspector about, if you decide that you would really like the house.

Solid Rock

A few housed are built directly on solid rock. In some areas, this is not too bad an idea: there is unlikely to be any trouble with settling, at least! In fact, one of my friends owns a 700-year-old house in Malta which is built this way; in this country, at least some of the houses on the Richmond Reninsula at Yorktown appear to be built the same way.

On the other hand, if there is the slightest risk of earthquakes, building on solid rock is a great way to make sure that a stone or brick house is reduced to powder as rapidly as possible. Rock transmits earthquake shocks very well indeed. A <u>frame</u> house on rock should shimmy and shake, but remain structurally sound; a masonry house will most likely be shaken to bits. This is unlikely to affect you at all, but if some seller tries to make a selling point out of the "bedrock" foundations, be aware that the advantages are not necessarily as great as they seem.

If You Can't See the Foundations

Sometimes, you may not be able to inspect the foundation walls directly. For example, if there is a proper basement (as distinct from a crawl space under the house), the walls may well have been covered with some sort of paneling. Also, you may decide that before you put on your overalls and start burrowing into crawl spaces (always assuming that they are accessible without tearing up the floors), you would rather take a more civilized look at the house. No problem!

In the outside check, you will already have seen whether there is any sagging in the outside walls: if there is, this can be a good indication that there are foundation problems. Next, indoors, check the interior walls and the floors. A floor that sags in the middle is indicative of sagging joists (see later section on Joists), but a floor which slopes is more likely the result of settled foundations.

It is surprising how much a house can "bend" without falling down — again, the medieval houses of Europe demonstrate this — and a good test of settling is by checking the smoothness with which doors and window sill open and close. If the house has settled somewhat, the door and window frames may no longer be "on the square", but may have become slightly "lozenged" or parallelogram-shaped. In extreme cases, you may even be able to see that the gap between the door and the frame above it is significantly wider at one end than at the other.

If the house has two stories, check the stairs: out-of-true stairs, or stairs that have pulled away from the wall, may well indicate problems with the foundation. If there are skirting boards (base boards or kick-boards) between the walls and the floor in any of the rooms, look at them. Are they "true," or are there signs of separation at the corners?

Don't Panic!

In the last section, I said that it is surprising how much a house can "bend;" and before we leave foundations, this is a point that is worth reinforcing. I have seen houses in many cities all over the world, which, at first sight, look as if they are falling down. In fact, there is a lovely story about the Temple Church in Bristol, in England. During World War Two, there was a heavy bombing raid near the church, and afterwards the wrecking crews went out to pull down dangerous structures. Only at the last minute were they persuaded to leave the tower of the Temple Church alone; the residents convinced them that although it appeared to be leaning at a dangerous angle, it had been like that for six hundred years.

("Balloon Frame / Platform Frame" Illustration)

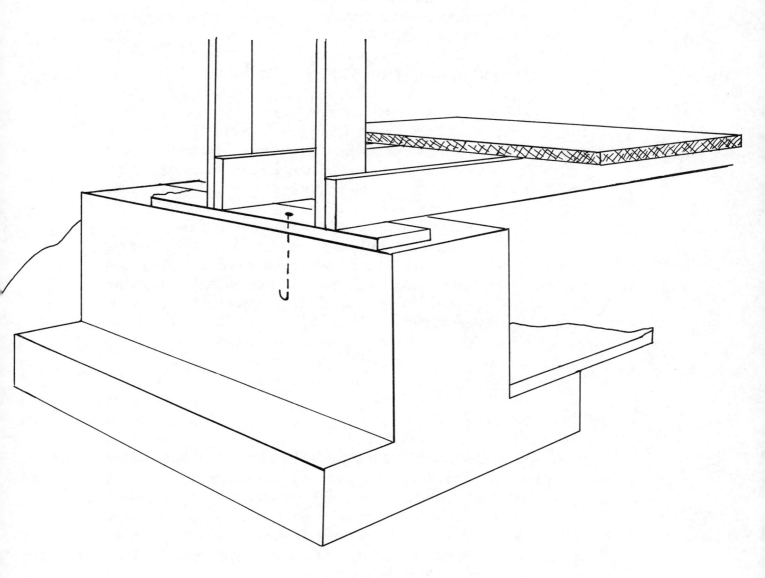

Figure C

My niece used to live in a place in San Francisco that had some distinctly odd angles; one of my favorite restaurants in Dover, Delaware, is certainly not made up entirely of right angles, and the house in which my wife was brought up was markedly "out of true" in places. If the house really has settled as far as it is going to settle, such things do not matter at all. On the other hand, you had better be *sure* that is has settled as far as it is gong to: I remember my parents looking at a house once where there was a *forty-foot* crack in one wall. At that point, who is going to risk it?

3.2   LOAD BEARING STRUCTURES

Once you have a good foundation, you can build a good house. In this country, most houses are of frame construction: that is, they are built of a wood frame which is then covered with a "skin" of outside and inside walls. This is common in countries where wood is plentiful and cheap, though in other countries brick, concrete, cinder-block or stone are much, much more common.

Although a frame house usually has a shorter life than a brick or stone house, it can still last for many hundreds of years. Provided that the builder did not take too many short cuts, an American frame house should last anything from about fifty to three or four hundred years. The picturesque timber-frame houses that we associate with Europe are made of much bigger, heavier timbers, and their means of construction is quite different, but there are many of these houses that have been standing for six or seven hundred years.

Platform Frame

The normal way of building a modern frame house is as a series of open "boxes." After the foundations have been laid, a sill plate is laid along the top and a sub-floor is laid on joists which lie on the sill plate. The house itself is then built as a single "box," open at top and bottom, and stands on top of the sub-floor. If it is a two-story house, another sub-floor is laid on top of this box, and a second open box is built on top of this. The roof is then laid on top of that.

("Typical Platform-Frame Construction" Illustration)

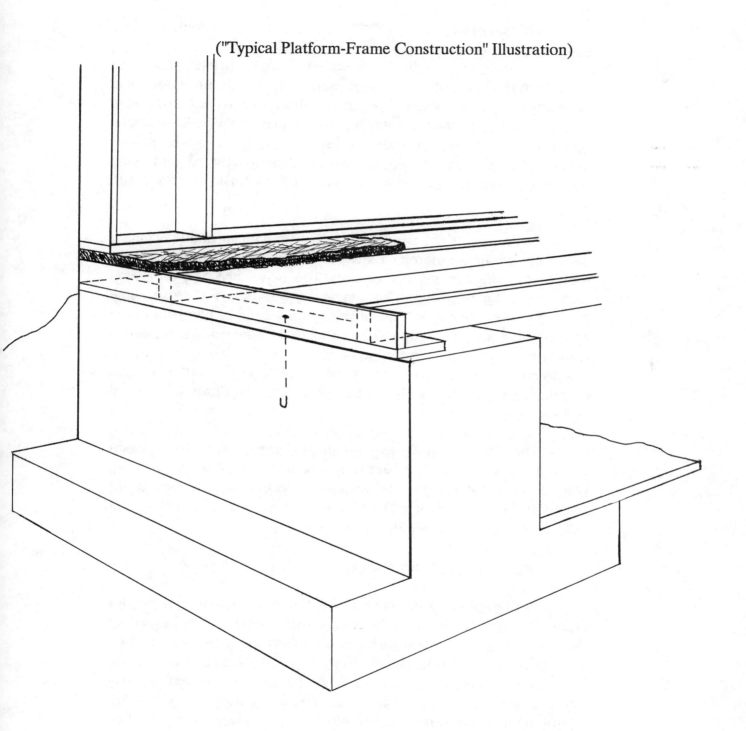

Figure D

58

Balloon Frame

Before about 1940, the so-called "balloon frame" was more usual than the platform frame. This used no sub-floor, but instead had very long studs (two-by-fours) which ran all the way from the sill plate to the rafters. The main reason for the decline of the balloon frame was fire regulations: obviously, a fire that started anywhere in a balloon-framed house could travel very rapidly upward and fairly rapidly downward. The platform frame, by contrast, creates a fire break at each floor.

Quite honestly, I would not worry very much about buying a balloon frame house merely because of the fire risk — though I might look at installing automatic sprinklers. This is just one of those things that is worth <u>knowing</u> about, but not worth <u>worrying</u> about. Also, some books give the impression that all frame houses are of platform frame construction, and this simply is not true. The difference it makes to inspecting the house is negligible — you are still going to inspect the woodwork and everything else in much the same way — but you might be puzzled if you did not know that there are two different types of construction.

The easiest way to explain the difference is with drawings, which is what I have done here. Figure C shows how similar the two types of construction are, and also shows you some common terms from the Glossary. Figures D and E are "close-ups" which show the differences rather than the similarities.

Other Types of Construction

With brick or stone construction, the main thing to look out for (apart from the condition of the walls themselves) is the places where the masonry and the woodwork meet. This is usually the most fruitful area for rot. On the other hand, if the masonry is sound, it is amazing how much rebuilding you can do. When I was a boy, I lived in a city where there was a whole terrace of twenty or thirty really big row homes, built of limestone. During World War II, these were gutted by fire when they were hit by a stick of incendiary bombs. After the war, they just put in new woodwork and did a minimum of work on the

("Typical Balloon-Frame Construction" Illustration)

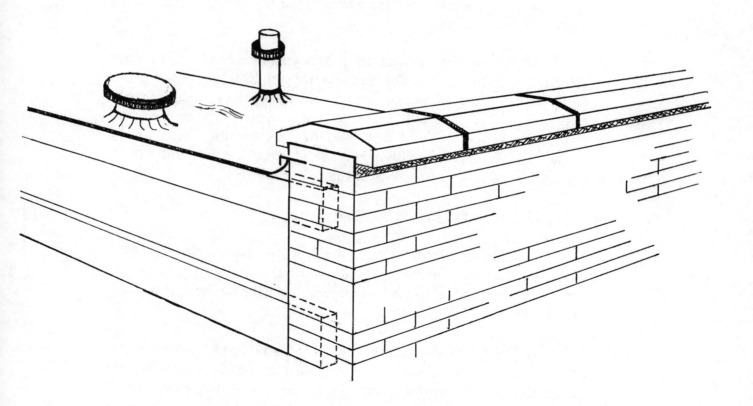

Figure E

masonry. Now, fifty and more years on, most people do not even know the homes were bombed.

3.3 ROOF STRUCTURE

The normal structure of a roof in this country is a ridge board (like the ridge pole of a tent) to which are fastened the sloping rafters. At their foot, the rafters are "tied together" by the roof joists, sometimes called roof beams. There may also be a "collar beam" running between the rafters: the purpose of this is to help resist the tendency of the "A" section of the roof to push the walls outwards, though it will also restrict the room available in the attic.

The most important thing to check is the condition of the ridge board (sometimes called the ridge beam), because replacing this is a very expensive undertaking: the whole of the rest of the roof has to be disassembled to replace it.

Look also for daylight (not impossible with tile roofs hung directly on battens) and for damage to (or "sistering" of) rafters. Damage to rafters is cheaper and easier to fix than damage to the ridge-board, but it is still a lot of work. "Sistering" (replacing or reinforcing rafters) should alert you to look for the cause of the damage, and for damage elsewhere; a "sistered" ridge-board can be grounds for rejecting the house outright.

If You Can't Get into the Roof

If there is no subflooring in the attic, you have a choice. Either you can get up into the roof and balance on the roof-joists as best you can, or you can try to do your inspection from the access hatch, using only a powerful flashlight.

In the rooms immediately below the attic level, look for water damage in the form of stains or (worse still) crumbling plaster. Do not accept the owner's assurance that the problem has been fixed without checking for yourself. Water stains may derive from the roof itself, or from overflowing guttering.

3.4 <u>FLOORS</u>

In some houses, especially in warm climates, floors may simply be the concrete pad on which the house is built. While this is acceptable in, say, southern California, it will make the house <u>very</u> expensive to heat in a colder climate. If you walk barefoot on stone or concrete, it feels cold because it conducts the heat away from your feet very rapidly. Wood, on the other hand, feels warm because it conducts the heat away very slowly.

This is why most houses have a wooden (or composite wood) floor which is supported on joists (see below). The air space beneath the joists serves two purposes. One is to keep the wood dry, because damp is the great enemy of wood, and the other is to provide additional insulation. The air should circulate under the floors, but it should not whistle under them!

<u>Joists</u>

Joists are floor-supporting beams which are typically spaced 16" apart (between centers). In some houses, they may be closer together than this, which is no problem (12" centers are a sign of first-class construction), but if they are further apart than 16", there is a danger that the floor will sag between the joists. This can mean anything from squeaks and slightly uneven flooring to a steadily deteriorating floor.

The maximum length of an unsupported joist is usually 16', and if the span is longer than this, there will usually be an additional beam which runs along under the joists, at right angles to them, dividing the span in two. This may be a heavy wood beam (more usual on older houses) or a steel girder. Either way, the beam may be supported by lally columns (see below). Alternatively, there may be an additional solid wall, in effect an extension of the foundations, which does the same job as the beam.

When inspecting joists, look for the following:

<u>Size</u> — Obviously, a joist must be big enough to do the job for which it was intended. Undersized joists are usually given away by "spongy" floors with a soft, "dead" feel; by sagging; and by generous

62

use of extra lally columns (see below) bearing directly on the joist. Normally, joists will be either 2x8 " or 2x10"; a Grade 1 joist of 2x8" is comparable with a Grade 2 in 2x10".

End fixing — As noted in the section on brick and stone-built houses, anywhere that wood meets masonry should be inspected closely. It is not unknown for the ends of joists to rot away completely so that the floors are holding <u>them</u> up, instead of vice versa, and the same problem is also encountered with the beams that run under the joists: sometimes, all that is holding these beams up is the lally columns.

In conventional frame construction, the joists rest <u>on</u> the sill plate, which in turn rests on the foundation: the sill plate is, therefore, the place to look for insect or water damage.

"Sistering" — As usual, replaced or reinforced joints should put you on your guard: what was wrong in the first place, and why was the original joist repaired, "sistered" (doubled) or replaced? Look for insect or water damage, or both.

Quality — Joists in any reasonably modern house will be stamped "Grade 1" or "Grade 2," and will be kiln-dried hem fir, Douglas fir or some other good building wood. If any of the joists bears a "Grade 3" stamp, it is of inferior quality; do not buy the house without an assurance from the building inspector that the joist is strong enough for the job.

Lally Columns

A lally column is (or should be) a vertical concrete-filled steel column that holds up the beam under the joists. Several lally columns may be used, and they should be evenly spaced; but sometimes, people move them to create more room and a more convenient working space. If the lally columns are very unevenly space, you should suspect that one (or more) may have been removed altogether, which could possibly compromise the integrity of the floor above. Often, you will be able to see traces of where the column used to stand before it was moved or taken away.

The reason I wrote "(or should be)" in the last paragraph is that some lally columns are of wood and others are of the requisite tubular steel construction, but are not concrete filled: hollow columns will "ring" when they are hit, while filled ones will give off a dull thud. In most jurisdictions, anything other than concrete-filled steel will not satisfy building codes, and will have to be replaced if the house is to be brought into conformity.

Insulation and Flooring

Insulation properly belongs in the next chapter, but it is worth mentioning that there should be a layer of insulation under the flooring: this will make the house much more comfortable to live in, and much more economical to heat.

The flooring material may be old-fashioned floorboards, or it may be some newer wood product, but either way, it should be flat, squeak-free and solid. Check near the edges of the room where water and insect damage are likeliest, if they are present at all.

Also, check the floor covering. If it is very new, be suspicious: what is it covering up? If the whole house has just had a "make-over," fair enough; but if there is a new carpet or some other form of floor covering in an otherwise shabby room, you have good cause to wonder what is underneath. Remember, too, that some types of flooring (such as parquet tiles) may look very attractive, but they also make it very hard to lift the floorboards. Modern houses are often better designed in this respect than older ones where plumbing and even wiring required major surgery to the floor, but it is still a point to consider.

3.5 ACCOMMODATIONS

I have divided the "accommodations" section into four groups. For the first, I have used a term that they use in Scotland, "public rooms." It sounds strange in English, but when you think about it, you realize that these are the rooms that people are most likely to see: the living room, the dining room (if the two are separate), the "family room," the "den" and so forth. It's much more accurate than the term "reception rooms."

Next come the bedrooms, third come the bathrooms, fourth the kitchen, and finally a brief note on fire escapes — not something we normally want to talk about, but still something that needs to be considered.

In all the rooms, you need to look out for the same basic things, as follows:

Plaster damage — At best, cracked or sagging plaster on the walls or ceiling means that you are going to have to do a "cover-up" job with drywall or replaster the room. At worst, it can be the symptom of a number of other faults, including problems with the studs, ceiling joists, or underlying material to which the plaster is anchored.

Diagonal crack around doors and windows — These mean either that the foundations are settling (or have settled) or that the frame is not properly constructed. It is debatable which is worse. Both can cost a fortune to fix.

Water stains — These may either result from water entry from the outside (defective guttering, bad shingling, roofing material missing, problems with the flashing) or from spillage inside, typically from bathrooms, but also sometimes from kitchens. Either way, they are bad news and you will need to reassure yourself that the problem has been cleared up, rather than just taking the owner's word for it.

Loose or damaged drywall — Exposed nail-heads, gaps or dents in the drywall, or exposed drywall jointing tape are not serious (though they look very bad), but the affected panels will need to be replaced or (more likely) patched with joint compound.

"Soggy" floors — As already mentioned, poor joists can lead to a floor that is sagging or just "dead" feeling. While this is one of those problems which might never get any worse, it is also one of those problems that is never going to get better on its own and it has the potential to get much worse. Carefully check the underlying joists if at all possible.

Public Rooms

There is not much extra to say about these, but there are a few points worth making:

Decor — Generally, shabby decor that needs replacement anyway is preferable to a sparkling new room which is totally out of tune with your tastes. In the first place, the owner is expecting you to pay for that hideous new paint job with the Technicolor carpet: he presumably likes it, and he may be surprised and even offended that you do not appreciate the "improvements" he has made to the house.

Shabbiness, on the other hand, is a good bargaining point. It also means that there is a better chance of getting the room the way you want it. I bought a house once that had an unbelievably hideous, but very high quality wool carpet in the sitting room. Because it was so new and of such high quality, I lived with it for a very long time, even though it was ugly. I just couldn't bring myself to throw out hardly-worn high-quality carpet!

Ease of redecoration — Look at the materials used for decorating. Too-thick old paint (common in older houses) will need to be removed if you want to re-paint properly. Wallpaper is much more trouble to strip off and replace than to paint over — and on some walls, you may find that there are several layers of paper, and maybe of paint as well. In one house, I stripped nine layers of paint and wallpaper off one wall! This is an extreme example, but it is not an unusual problem.

"Livability" — Imagine yourself living in that room. Will your furniture fit? Will your *lifestyle* fit? My brother lives in a very inexpensive house that I would only take as a gift. The layout — the doors and windows, the location, the lighting, everything — just would not suit the way that my wife and I live.

Look out for awkwardly placed doors. One of my friends lives in a house where you cannot get into the kitchen if the door between the kitchen and the garage is open. If you have teenage children, do they have to go through the living room to get to their rooms? On the one hand, it helps you to keep tabs on them, on the other hand, it can turn the room into a corridor and a constant source of family fights.

If the kitchen and the dining room are a long way apart (assuming they are separate and you decide to keep them that way), how will it be if you have friends over to eat? In the past, houses were often designed on the assumption that cooking would be taken care of by a servant (if you were rich) or by the wife (if you weren't). In a modern family where both spouses might work, this kind of separation is no longer acceptable.

Security — Great big French windows may look good, but if they can be lifted straight out of their frames (see section on Doors and Door Glazing in Chapter 2), they are not too good for security.

Privacy — Does the living room look out onto the street, or onto a side garden? You may prefer not to live your life in a goldfish bowl.

Insulation — This is dealt with in the next chapter, but it's still worth checking as you look through the rooms. You are going to be spending a lot of time in this room if you buy this house. If the room is drafty and cold, you will be spending a lot of money on it too.

Fireplaces and Chimneys — Look up the chimney flue with a <u>powerful</u> flashlight (and consider a shower cap to protect your hair!). You are looking for a sound chimney lining and for build-ups of tar or creosote in the chimney.

Check the condition of the brickwork and also of the damper in the flue; it should be possible to close this tightly so that when you are not using the fireplace, the chimney is not a source of draughts.

Bedrooms

Many of the same comments apply to bedrooms as to public rooms, but there are a couple of things to watch out for.

Size — Many times, I have been shown a "three bedroom" or "four bedroom" house where one of the bedrooms was little more than a large closet — the sort of thing that used to be called a box room. You might be able to put a young (pre-teen) child into it, but that is all. In one such room, there was a built-in bed. It looked good until you took a tape-measure to it and found that the reason it was built in was that it was only six feet long, significantly shorter than most "real" beds.

"Walk-throughs" — Sometimes, one of the "bedrooms" is the only means of access to the guest bathroom or (in one or two cases that I have seen, the *only* bathroom. As already mentioned, this severely limits its usefulness.

Bathrooms

In some areas, chipped or cracked bathroom fittings (washbasins, toilet, or even shower stalls) are violations of the building code. This may seem unutterably trivial, until the company financing your house tells you that the building has to be brought into conformity with the code within (say) six months, or they will cut off the mortgage.

It may seem "penny-ante," but it is a good idea to check that everything in the bathroom actually *works*. Fill the sink with the plug in it; check that both the hot and the cold tap operate smoothly, without spitting or snorting. Let the sink drain. Look for leaks and listen for loud gurgling sounds which may indicate a blocked (or never-installed) vent. Building codes require that *all* drains be vented to prevent "blow-backs" due to sewer gas (methane) in the system. If you have ever seen (and smelled) a bad blow-back, you will know why venting is important. Somewhere, there should be at least one vent that projects above roof level.

Check the bath the same way (you an use mostly cold water). Is there enough water pressure to fill the bath reasonably quickly, or is it one of those places where you go and watch your favorite TV program for an hour while the bath fills? And does the bath empty quickly? We have all been in places where a torrent of water comes out of either tap, but where it takes half an hour for the bath water to drain away. Check the shower, too.

Try to rock the toilet. It should be bolted firmly to the floor. Check the joint behind the bowl, especially if he toilet is not rock-steady. This is a typical place for a small, maddening, and hard-to-fix leak. Also, look for dampness around the base. Work the flush. Does it work first time, then refill *and cut off* smartly and quietly? Check for leaks once again. This is not the most pleasant part of inspecting the house, but it is better to learn about it now rather than after you have bought the house. Look for water stains in rooms below the bathroom(s).

If the bathroom has been modernized, this can be a mixed blessing. Done well, it adds to the value of the house and makes it more agreeable to live in. Done badly, it can introduce problems (poor drainage, leaks, wiring too near water supplies) which were not there in the original, "old-fashioned" bathroom.

If the bathroom is *really* old-fashioned, remember that cast-iron baths with ball and claw feet and porcelain-handled brass taps are, if they are in good condition, surprisingly valuable. So are colored toilet bowls. Don't just smash them up or tell the contractor that he can have them for nothing when he puts in a new bathroom suite!

Kitchen

A really comfortable kitchen can be the most important room in the house, a center for the whole family. On the other hand, don't get carried away with the idea that the kitchen is the only family room.

Your expectations of a kitchen will depend very much on your lifestyle, too. If you have aspirations towards *cordon bleu* you will want a kitchen in which you can create your art. If you are of the grab-it-on-the-run persuasion, you will need a big refrigerator/freezer and a microwave oven. If you have children who never have time for a meal, but always have time for a snack, you will need a big kitchen table and a well-stocked refrigerator (and maybe a big cookie jar).

If you use lots of electrical appliances — food processors, blenders, can openers, spice or coffee grinders, toasters, microwave ovens, coffee makers and more — you had better make sure that the kitchen has plenty of readily accessible electric outlets.

Ask which appliances are included in the sale of the house. Don't just assume that the dishwasher and the refrigerator and the stove are included in the deal. They probably are, but it never hurts to check. All you need to say is something like. "I suppose the dishwasher and the refrigerator and the stove will stay behind when you move?" Different people have different expectations and may try to charge you extra for these things if it is not agreed beforehand that they are a part of the deal.

As with the bathroom fittings, a chipped kitchen sink is considered to be in violation of building codes in some jurisdictions, so be aware that you may be required to replace this before you can get final mortgage approval. Test the sink (filling and emptying) and look for shut-off valves on both the hot and cold water lines under the sink.

Check the heating and cooling and ventilation: a too-cold kitchen is rarer than one that is too hot, but it should be possible to be cosy on a cold day when you are cooking nothing, or cool enough to work on a hot day when you are using every burner, the oven and quite possibly the broiler as well.

The Kitchen "Triangle" — No, this isn't a relative of the Bermuda Triangle, though you may sometimes feel that way about the kitchen. Instead, it's the rule governing the layout of the oven, the sink, and the main working surface or counter-top. Generally, they should be arranged so that if you draw a line from one to the other, you move in a triangle with roughly equal sides. If one side is much longer than the other, or worse still, if you have to go around a corner or into another room (a utility room, for example) to get to the refrigerator, the kitchen will be slow and frustrating to work in.

Kitchen Decor — Like living room decor, this is extremely personal and you have a simple choice. You can live with someone else's taste, whether it is new or old, or you can lay out money to make the kitchen over into what you want.

This is where there is a lot to be said for buying a house which, if it is not actually a "fixer-upper," is at least slightly shabby. Then, when you remodel, you can start with a clear conscience (because it had to be done anyway) and build the kitchen that *you* want.

Do not neglect the value a coat of paint can have, even if it is only a temporary measure until you can afford the makeover that you want, but equally, ask yourself if you can *really* work in a kitchen where the counter tops are worn, stained or dirty looking.

It is also worth mentioning that a "dream kitchen" is still one of the strongest selling points that a house can have. If you buy a house that already has a "dream kitchen," you may well find that you are paying rather "over the odds" for a kitchen that is not *quite* what you want. A shabby kitchen, on the other hand, can knock several thousand off the price of a house — maybe more than it would cost to build exactly the kitchen that you *do* want! In your turn, when you come to sell the house, you will find that a well-refitted kitchen will repay the investment you made, both in the enhanced value of the house and in the extra speed with which you can sell it.

Fire Escapes

It is not particularly important what *sort* of fire escapes the house has, it is merely important that in the case of fire, you should be able to get out quickly and safely. This is where excessive security (such as grilles on windows and doors, unless fitted with quick release bars) becomes a drawback instead of a help. In each room in turn, ask yourself a simple question, "What would I do *now* if somebody yelled FIRE?"

If the answer is not as immediately obvious as the question, you need to think twice about the safety of the room you are in. By way of experiment, I asked myself exactly this question in the room where I typed this. The answer was simple. It's a ground-floor room with a big window. All I would have to do is climb over my desk and jump through the screen.

If the building you are looking at is tall enough to have regular, external fire escapes, you should check the general structural integrity of the steelwork; the anchorage points where the fire escape is fixed to the wall (an area that is frequently corroded) and try the mechanism which lowers the ladder from the second floor to the ground. For obvious security reasons, the last stage (from the second floor to the ground) is normally on some kind of a "drawbridge" so that it can be quickly raised or lowered.

In some jurisdictions, a fire escape that shows signs of rust is a violation of the building code — but you should also be aware of the risks of over-enthusiastic painting. I have seen winch mechanisms that have been painted over so many times that they are locked solid and would require several hours of chipping away old paint before they could be used.

3.6   STORAGE

One of the great problems about putting down roots is the sheer quantity of possessions you accumulate — and you have to put them somewhere! I used to know one man who reckoned that he always moved, every two years, in order to avoid gaining too many possessions. Anything that he could not carry in his own pickup truck in one journey, he gave away or sold. It wasn't a very big pickup truck, either -— but you should have seen how high he could pile it!

Garage

At the very least, you store your car in the garage. If you are like many people, though, there is no room for the car. You have too many other things to store in there!

If the garage is free-standing, or shares only one wall of the house, the rules for examining it are much the same as for examining the house itself: look for cracks in the walls and deterioration in he woodwork, including the rafters and the door surround. Check the roof: for some reason, people often forget or neglect to re-cover a garage roof when they have the roof of the main house re-covered. Check the condition of the floor slab: if it is badly cracked, pouring new one will be expensive.

In some jurisdictions, wooden garages are a violation of the building code. This is based on the somewhat dubious argument that a wooden garage is a greater fire risk than, say, a wooden kitchen: mortgage and insurance companies seem to still be living in the early part of this century, when automobiles were regarded as dangerous, unpredictable things which might suddenly burst into flames at any time. Also, *integral* garages that are part of a wooden house appear to be no problem — though logically, it would seem that they were *more* of a problem than free-standing garages which are much less likely to set the whole house afire.

In an integral garage, the interior construction materials and the door between the garage and the house must, however, be "fire-rated"; that is to say, treated with fire-retarding chemicals.

Whether the garage is free-standing or integral, check that the door opens and closes freely; that it can be locked securely; and (if it is automatic) that the auto-stop works. Check the last by trying to stop the door as it descends, leaving yourself plenty of room to get out of the way. When the door encounters resistance, it should not just stop: it should actually go back up again. If the auto-stop is defective, a garage door is heavy enough to squash pets and even small children: keep this in mind!

Attic

The things that you will need to check in an attic will vary, according to whether the roof-space is being used as a living space (whether built or adapted that way) or whether it is "unfinished" — in other words, jut an empty space. If the house has a flat roof, there is normally a space between the ceiling of the uppermost room and the roof which is called a "cock loft." This is also dealt with below.

One thing that you need to check in *any* attic or cock loft is venting. All this means is that there must be a means for air to circulate easily, without actually whistling through like a wind. If the air cannot circulate, there is a danger of moisture building up in the "dead air" space, with the usual ill effects on the timber roof joists or even on the rafters and ridge board. You might think that if the space really is sealed, moisture could not build up; but the answer is that the seal is never perfect, and moisture always finds it easier to get *in* than to get *out*.

In a conventional unfinished attic, traditional venting is via a ridge vent along the top of the roof, plus vented soffits; soffits are the bit between the eaves and the house. Alternatively, there may be a roof vent (like a little tin chimney with a with a conical "hat" on top or with louvred sides) or a vent window. If there is no venting, be extra-vigilant when it comes to checking for moisture damage in the roof timbers. Use your nose, too: there may be a musty smell which indicates no venting and possible moisture damage.

Unfinished Attics — The first thing to check in an unfinished attic is the insulation. This may be roll-type (glass fibre), "rock wool" (a bit like fire-resistant flock or kapok), or vermiculite, which is a sort of expanded mica in the form of coarse granules; this is just poured between the roof-joists. The bare minimum of insulation that is up there should be about four inches: six or eight inches is better; and twelve inches is not too much.

There should be a single vapor barrier between the living accommodation and the roof space; additional vapor barriers are an invitation to condensation between the two layers, which can in time build up enough to damage the roof joists.

Attics Used as Living Space — With these, the insulation must be between the drywall that covers the rafters and the roof sheathing itself. The insulation should *not*, however, fill the entire space: there must be room for air to circulate, via vented soffits and a ridge vent.

Cock Lofts — The cock loft not only serves as a space for air to circulate, it is also a very effective insulator in its own right. If there is no vent, though, the air in the cock loft can become very hot indeed in summer, and this will, in turn, raise the temperature of the rooms immediately below.

Cellar

Cellars are extremely useful, but they also introduce a number of problems, most of which are associated with dampness.

The worst is if the cellar is below the water table, as described in Section 1.2. In this case, the only sound advice is to look for another house.

Look for water stains. If there are many, the chances are the cellar has flooded — perhaps more than once. This has happened in my aunt's house in Delaware. If you are lucky, the flooding is only the result of a storm drain blocking up, often because of a tree root. If you are unlucky, there may be serious problems with mains drainage, including sewers. That can be *very* unpleasant indeed. The only way to find out about this is to ask some hard questions of the owner. In a few areas, the problem lies not with the house, but with the town's whole sewage system, or at least with the sewage system in a given area. Either avoid that area altogether, or consider only houses which have no cellars if you particularly want to live there.

Look for a sump pump. This is an admission that water is a problem, and once again invites tough questioning. You may care to uncover the sump pit — the manhole cover that gives access to the main drainage — to see if there is evidence if frequent risings of the waters.

Even in a well-drained area, there can be problems with dampness. For example, a drainpipe that is not led or directed away from the wall can lead to moisture problems, although these are, for the most part, quickly and easily solved.

Of course, *no* cellar is likely to be bone dry, and you have to balance the amount and kind of moisture against the convenience of the cellar and the other advantages of the house. A dehumidifier can make all the difference in some cellars, drying the air enough to remove the musty smell, though natural ventilation is preferable if you can get it. Check the bottom of the drywall that has been used to line the cellar to see if it is obviously moisture-damaged.

Remember that it is possible (though extremely expensive) to have a moderately damp cellar waterproofed by excavating the foundation wall and re-waterproofing that. There are other waterproofing techniques, but they are less effective.

Crawl Spaces

In many houses, there will be a crawl space that is accessible from the cellar. This goes under the floors and gives you an opportunity to examine the joists in detail. The crawl space is normally only a couple of feet high, so it is not a place to venture into if you are claustrophobic, but you should at least shine your flashlight in there. An important thing to note in the crawl space is whether the dirt is covered or uncovered: bare earth should be covered with a vapor barrier (plastic sheeting is fine) to prevent moisture buildup and condensation on the floor joists.

Outbuildings

There is not much to say about outbuildings: basically, you want the same degree of structural integrity and freedom from rot that you would look for in the house itself, or that you would expect in a separate garage. Of course, all of the buildings should have been constructed with building permits (where applicable) and in conformity with building codes. If no permits were obtained, you may be liable for paying for the permits later (together with penalties), and if the buildings are not in conformity with building codes, you may be required to demolish and remove them altogether! So if the owner touts an "addition" he did, or if you are looking at a tract house that *obviously* has an extra outbuilding (or, say, an apartment over the garage) that the neighbors don't have, ask to see the permits and the "okay" given by the city building inspector before you even **consider** buying this house.

Look out, too, for outbuildings which are in dangerous condition; this sometimes happens in country properties, where a little-used building is allowed to deteriorate. All you need is for one child — who need not even be on your property with your permission — to be injured, and you are in for a heavy lawsuit. Or, of course, you may have

76

("Crawl Space with Vapor Barrier" Illustration)

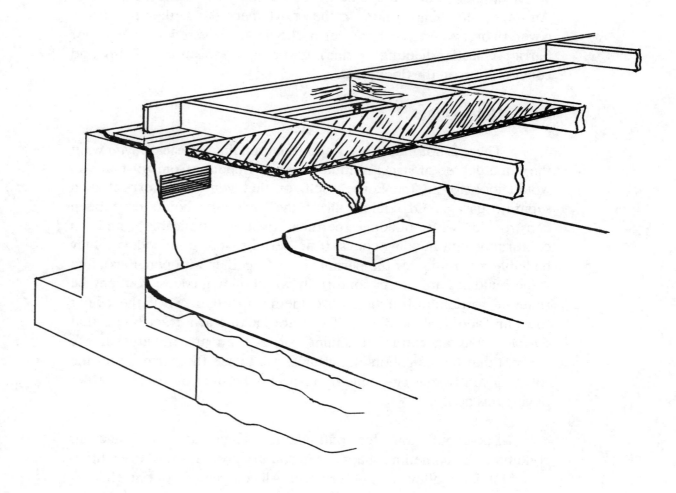

Figure F

children of your own. Make sure that the price of the house reflects the cost of either pulling down, or making good, an unsafe outbuilding.

Remember that in a greenhouse, direct light is greatly preferable to help the plants grow, while in a sun room, diffused lighting is more pleasant.

Finally, check that there is nothing nasty lurking in the outbuildings. A friend of mine once found some old, sweating gelignite in an outbuilding on her grandfather's farm. She and her brother used to play with it. To this day, she is amazed that she survived.

4.0   <u>SYSTEMS AND SERVICES</u>

So: you know how to make sure that a house is structurally sound. You have done the most difficult bit. Just about anything else can be fixed, usually comparatively easily and often reasonably affordable.

Even so, if you have spent this much time and effort checking the house over, you might as well make sure that the other features and systems of the house are *perfect* — or if not perfect, then at least in excellent condition. Taken individually, it may not cost all that much to have a new water heater put in, or to install a security system or smoke detectors, or to add insulation, or even to have the place rewired. Certainly, none of these things would be as disruptive as having the roof timbers renewed, or the foundations waterproofed.

Put them all together, though, and the cost can add up surprisingly quickly. At the risk of sounding like a killjoy, owning your own house can expose you to expenses you had probably never given a thought before — such as replacing a central heating boiler.

Fortunately, there is a bright side to all this. Suppose you need (say) a new water heater, and that it would cost (say) $400 to buy it and have it installed — I'm just using round numbers. You say to the house owner, "Getting a new water heater is going to cost close to $500, without taking account of the mess and disruption while they're doing it. Do you want to have a new one put in, or do you want to knock $500 off the price of the house, and I'll do it?

The chances are that he'll let you do it. It has cost you literally *nothing*, except a small amount of bother while it is actually installed.

The same would go for re-wiring, or a new air conditioner, or whatever. If there are several faults, don't haggle over each one. Instead, add up what you guess it would cost to fix them all (or get estimates); add on fifty percent; and once again, make your offer. Let's say you reckon it would cost $2000 to fix a number of faults. Add on fifty percent, and that's $3000. The add-on is because such jobs rarely come in *under* budget, and besides, you are the one that is going to be inconvenienced. The seller is getting away without trouble. You might then say, "Well, I reckon it needs about three thousand dollars spent. You're asking $95,000. I don't think the house is worth that much, even in perfect condition, and I think you'll agree that the house isn't quite that good. If everything was all right, I might go to $90,000; but with these faults, I really don't think it's worth more than $85.000."

You may dicker a bit, and end up agreeing on $87,000, but that still represents the difference between the $90,000 you were willing to pay for a house in good condition and the cost of installing the new water heater, wiring, or whatever. In other words, you reckon to end up paying the *same* for new, guaranteed goods as you would have paid for used goods if they had been in good condition.

On the other hand, do not get too excited over minor details. So the refrigerator needs replacing — so what? Sure, it's $500 or so, but unless the seller is trying to make a big deal out of the fact that he is leaving a load of worn-out junk behind (the refrigerator, the stove, the dishwasher ...) you should not make much of it, either. What you are concerned with is the fabric of the house: the plumbing, the mains supplies, the heating, and so forth.

4.1 WATER

A few years back, I heard a lovely story. An old woman, born in the last century, was admiring her granddaughter's new kitchen. Her eyes twinkled as she said, "It sure is different from the kitchen I had when I was your age. You've got all these wonderful new conveniences — tell me, which one do you think is the best of all?" The young woman though. "I don't know," she said. "The microwave ... the self-cleaning stove ... no, it must be the refrigerator ... why? What would you say?" The older woman chuckled. "I'd take running water every time."

Of course, we mostly take water for granted today. Remember, though, that not all water is mains water. Many farms still have their own wells. In Bermuda, we used to drink rainwater that we collected off the roof. And I knew one remote farm where the water came off a cliff, and you would occasionally get bits of leaf in a glass of water. Water bears more thinking about than you may have imagined.

Main Supply

While you can generally rely on the local water company to provide a good main pipe, the connection between the main and your home is your responsibility. In older houses, there is a considerable likelihood that the connection will be lead, which is not desirable.

The biggest objection is that lead in the water is *extremely* bad for you. For all the hoo-hah surrounding leaded gasoline, lead pipes are far, far worse when it comes to introducing lead into your system, and the vast majority of people with high lead levels in their bodies got it from drinking water, not from gasoline emissions. When you realize that this translates directly into brain damage in children, and a number of other complications for adults, you do *not* want lead pipes. Modern houses use copper.

A smaller objection is that old lead pipe connections can, and sometimes do, burst. It is not nearly as common as some people would have you believe, but with replacement costs running at a minimum of about $1000, and quite possible two or three times as much, it's not a risk you want to take — especially along with the lead poisoning. The expense is, however, the reason why there are so many lead mains connections still around.

There should be a mains shut-off valve which isolates the house from the mains supply, and it should be in good working order. They very rarely fail, at least in any area where I have lived, though apparently there are parts of the country where they refuse to work as often as not.

There may or may not be a drain valve near the shut-off valve. This is used to drain the house plumbing completely (after the shut-off valve has been closed!) for major plumbing work; but in practice, you can usually drain the house system sufficiently, simply by using the bath, sink and (especially) hose or sprinkler faucets.

The water main also provides the ground for the electrical supply box (bus box, junction box, panel box, breaker box, mains box, power box — it goes under many different names), and you should check this connection when you are checking the water. An ungrounded electrical system can be *very* dangerous.

Cold-Water System

Once again, watch out for lead piping. The modern alternative is copper, which is very much better (lighter, strong, and *much* better for you), but plastics are used increasingly; occasionally you may even find a little stainless steel, especially for flexible connectors.

There are various grades of "copper" piping, including the so-called "yellow brass" and "red brass" which are both inferior copper alloys. At its best, "red brass" is effectively copper, but "yellow brass" is inclined to corrode. If you are ordering replacement piping, order copper.

In some houses, especially those built in the 1930s, you may also find galvanized steel piping. While this is not much of a health risk, it is very prone to corrosion and to clogging. If a house has been shut up for a while, and rusty-looking water comes out of the faucets when you try them, there is almost certainly galvanized iron piping somewhere.

If the house has lead or "yellow" brass" or galvanized piping, you would be *very* wise to replace it before it either affects your health (lead only) or bursts. The expense may be painful, but the expense of replacing ruined furnishings *as well as* pipes, and of doing it on an emergency basis, will be even more painful. If some of the pipes have been replaced with copper and others have not, you can safely bet that the pipes that have *not* been replaced will need to be replaced soon.

In cold climates, the pipes should be run in a way that reduces the likelihood of their freezing. If your area is not subject to very cold winters, then simply lagging (insulating) the pipes may be sufficient. In areas where it gets very cold, though, the pipes should not pass through unheated areas.

Hot Water

The hot water system will have its own network of pipes, which you can conveniently check at the same time as you check the cold water pipes. Here, we are more concerned with the means of heating the water; the distance from the water heater to the faucets; and the insulation of the pipes.

At the time of writing, mains gas was the cheapest way to heat water — about half as much as electricity — and oil was somewhere between gas and electricity, though obviously subject to wide fluctuations.

Although combined hot water/central heating boilers are superficially attractive, and indeed make sense wherever you need to use the central heating for much of the year, it is usually *more* energy efficient to keep the water heater and the central heating boiler separate. If you live someplace where you do not use the heating much, separating the two is certainly much more efficient.

The life of a water heater is surprisingly short — about 8-10 years. After that, they start to leak, fill up with crud ("Corrosion Residue and Undetermined Detritus"), and generally misbehave. Ask the owner how old the unit is. Ask if the heater has ever been drained or flushed; this can considerably increase its life. Look for a pressure safety valve and lead-off: if there is no safety valve, and the tank overheats (for example because of a faulty thermostat), it can explode, with dire consequences. The pressure safety valve ensures that it will vent before it explodes; the lead-off from the pressure safety valve ensures that the scalding water and steam will be directed down to the floor, rather than spraying out at whoever may be in the area at the time.

Ideally, you want at least a 50- or 60-gallon water heater: 40 gallons is just sufficient, and 30 gallons is inconveniently small — one deep, hot bath can leave you without adequate hot water for half an hour or more. The water heater tank should also be well insulated, especially in cold climates: heat losses through the wall of the tank will be significant otherwise. This is why the recovery rate figures on the front of the tank (telling you how many gallons of water the tank can heat in one hour) are no more than a general guideline.

If the house is equipped with a combination central heating boiler and water heater, examine the places where the water heating coils enter the boiler for signs of rust, or water spots; these could indicate that the water-heating part is not long for this world.

With any type of water heater, check all connections for signs of corrosion — corroded connections are a strong indication that the unit may need replacing in the near future — and with gas or oil fired units, check the flue which leads the combustion bases out of the house. A faulty flue can leak carbon dioxide and (much worse) carbon monoxide into the house; sufficient build-ups of either, but especially of carbon monoxide, can be deadly.

The water heater should be reasonably close to the faucets. A faucet that is at the opposite end of the house from the water heater will take a long time to warm up, wasting both heat and water as it does so. Also, the hot-water pipes will lose much less heat if they are lagged or otherwise insulated: on a cold day, with a long pipe-run, water might start out at 160° at the tank, but cool to 100-110° before it reaches the faucet. This is not just a waste of water and heat, it is a real nuisance if you are expecting piping-hot water out of the tap!

Water Softeners

The value of water softeners is questionable. Many are ecologically unsound and, at best, most of them operate by converting insoluble minerals (the ones that cause "fur" or mineral deposits) into soluble ones, so that water is no better for you, it just has a different set of chemicals dissolved in it. Also, softened water has a very high sodium content, which is not good for anyone and is best avoided, on medical advice, by many people.

In areas where the water is very hard, though, a water softener will undoubtedly make life more convenient; you will not need to de-scale coffee makers as often, the dishwasher will leave fewer spots on the glasses, and so forth. You may, however, find that bottled water (buy the big 5-gallon variety) is more palatable and more ecologically acceptable for drinking, while the water softener (if you *must* have one) can be connected only to the hot-water plumbing, where scale and other deposits are more of a problem.

4.2   DRAINAGE

The three most common materials for drain lines are galvanized steel, cast iron and plastic. Some areas still consider plastic to be a violation of building codes — a pretty stone-age view, but it is worth checking the regulations in your area.

If the house has iron pipes, look out for corrosion, and look to see if some sections are newer than others; as usual, if one part has been replaced, it is likely that other parts will also have to be replaced soon.

The drainage system should be vented, with a vent stack above roof level. Often, especially in a two-story house, this vent stack is a continuation of the main down-pipe. The main down-pipe is typically a 4-inch pipe into which all the other pipes — from sinks, baths, toilets, dishwashers, etc. — empty. The vent stack is *essential*: so-called "sewer gas" is mainly methane which, when mixed with air in the right proportions is very explosive indeed. A major sewer-gas explosion can reduce a house to matchwood. Fortunately, methane is lighter than air, and will discharge harmlessly through a vent stack.

If a bath or sink is slow-draining, the chances are that the blockage is in the U-trap under the sink. This U-trap, which is permanently full of water and prevents the return of sewer gas through the drain, can collect muck and debris, which is why it is normally fitted with a drain plug at the bottom of the U. Removing the drain-plug can be a stomach-turning job, and you will need to use some sort of sealant (PTFE tape is good) to make sure that it does not leak when you replace it, but it is not a difficult job. Of course, check to see that U-traps (or P-traps, a similar design in bathrooms) are not leaking already.

Mains Drainage

The thing to look out for with mains drainage is tree roots getting into your drains between the house and the city mains. Slow-emptying bathtubs are one indication of this, though, as already noted, the problem in that case is more likely to be local. A better indicator of problems is water-marks or even silt from back-up drain lines. Some people call a drain-clearing company *every year* to clean their drains — Roto-Rooter is one of the best known names — but every 2-5 years is generally adequate. After all, tree roots do not grow very fast: if you inspect the main drainage sump once a year, and see that water is flowing through it freely (have someone flush the toilets and empty the bath, while you are looking), there are unlikely to be any problems.

Septic Tanks

There are many kinds of septic tanks. A properly-designed one will last for decades with absolutely no maintenance, but it must be *big, well designed and well made.* An inferior septic tank system can require frequent pumping out, which is quite expensive and smells quite unpleasant. If you have your doubts, ask the neighbors if there have been any problems with the house you are looking at. They will almost certainly have noticed if there are!

To minimize problems with septic tanks, avoid sending the following materials into them: oils, greases and fats, or strong chemicals (such as photographic chemicals, drain cleaners, or even large quantities of bleach), as these will kill or inhibit the bacteria that break up the waste.

If you decide that you might like to buy a house without mains drainage, the reliable operation of the septic tank is one of the points on which you want specific reassurance from the professional building inspector whom you hire to inspect the building.

4.3   ELECTRICITY

"You can't see it, and it bites." I have always liked this description of electricity, which I owe to my father, a marine engineer who is happier with steam than with electricity.

Not only does it bite, though: it also has the potential to cause fires. This is why it is highly advisable to check the electrical arrangements in any house *very carefully indeed.*

Main Supply

Unlike most of the world, the United States uses the relatively inefficient 110-125 volt supply to drive most appliances: in Europe, 220-250 volt supplies are more common. The higher voltage allows for smaller, more energy-efficient motors and lighter switch gear, because doubling the *voltage* required means that you halve the *current* required. The drawback to the higher voltage is that it is more dangerous: a 110-volt shock is uncomfortable, but rarely dangerous, while a 240-volt shock can, in the wrong conditions, be lethal.

In fact, distribution from the local substation to the house is normally at 220-250 volts, which is then broken down into 110-125 volts at the junction box where the power comes into the house. This means that almost all houses have the potential for a 220-250 volt supply (the precise voltage varies from area to area), though some modern houses — especially cheaper modern houses — are wired only for the lower voltage. In the house I live in now, I had to pay almost $400 to have 240-volt supplies put in for the clothes-dryer and for other appliances.

A measure of the power available in the house is the *amperage* of the supply. Older houses, where electricity was originally used only for lighting and for a few small appliances such as electric irons and electric fans, may have a supply that is as low as 30 amps. This allows only 3300 watts (3.3 kilowatts, or Kw) of electrical appliances to be used at any one time — a watt is a measure of electrical consumption — and this is woefully inadequate for a modern house: a clothes dryer can easily be 2 to 3 Kw, and an electric water heater can be 5 Kw or more. If you turn on more appliances than the supply can handle, you will blow the fuses or trip the circuit breakers.

As I look around me, I can see 600W of lighting; over 1000W of computers and printers; 100W of telephones and telephone-answering machines; and about 200W of other electrical equipment. Add them all together, and you have close to 2000W (2 Kw) — and that's only in one room, where in winter I might also have a 1200W (1.2 Kw) electric heater!

Most modern houses have at least 100 amps on tap, which allows you to run 11,000 watts (11 Kw) of appliances simultaneously —

and even that might be on the modest side if you have an electric water heater and a powerful central air-conditioning system. The amperage of the house supply will usually be marked on the junction box; if it is not, each individual circuit breaker in the box should be marked, and you can quickly add the values together to discover the total power available.

The "quality" of electricity varies widely. In some areas, the supply is very rarely interrupted, always stays close to the nominal voltage, and is not troubled with "spikes," "surges" and "brown-outs." In other areas, all of these troubles are commonplace.

As a rule, underground power supplies are more reliable than above-ground power supplies, especially during thunderstorms and high winds.

If you own expensive computers, hi-fi, etc., and the local supply is not "clean," you may wish to protect your investment with "spike suppressors" (available from all good electronics stores), "line conditioners" (a more expensive version of the same thing), or even "uninterruptible power supplies" (UPS), which provide a battery back-up in the case of mains failure.

Wiring

Unfortunately, wiring is one of those things which seems to attract enthusiastic amateurs. While it is perfectly possible for an amateur to install safe wiring that complies with building codes, it is also perfectly possible for an amateur to make a nightmarish mess of the whole thing. If the owner of the house says, "I put this in myself," then alarm bells should start ringing in your head. If there seem to be unusually high numbers of outlets for an older house, or if the outlets are in unusual places, you should ask who put them in, and when.

If the house has an old 30-amp or even 60-amp supply, you are unlikely to have enough power outlets, and it is not just a matter of adding more outlets; you will have to upgrade the whole wiring system as well. This is not cheap. On the other hand, a newer system is generally safer than an older one, both because of the reduced risk of electric shocks (grounding on older systems was sometimes rather casual) and because of the reduced fire risk.

One VERY important thing to look out for is aluminum wiring. This is a terrifyingly dangerous cost-cutting measure which is no longer legal in many areas: aluminum wires corrode and rapidly become a fire hazard. Even if aluminum wiring still permitted by the building codes in your area (which it should not be), you would be very unwise not to have it replaced with copper if you buy the house.

Electrical Systems

I have already mentioned electrical water heaters, and if there are other appliances included in the sale of the house (dishwashers, clothes dryers, refrigerators, etc.), you should check that they are in good condition. The wiring should be clean and sound, and the appliance should look as if it still has some life left in it: it makes no sense to give house room to an appliance that is on its last legs. As I said before, though, if they are not in good condition, they add nothing to the value of the house and take nothing away from it: only when the seller is saying, "but look at this beautifully-fitted kitchen! is it appropriate to point out that most of it will have to be replaced in a couple of years anyway. Another point about appliances left behind: if they really are unusable, you may wish to be sure the seller will dispose of them when he leaves — having large appliances hauled away can be very expensive.

The big item, and the one that you do need to check, is electric heating. Although this is clean and relatively maintenance-free, it is easily the most expensive way to heat a house. Electric central heating systems (forced-air, "hot floor" with heating elements embedded in concrete, or "night storage" where cheap off-peak nighttime electricity is used to heat concrete blocks which then give off their heat during the day) are theoretically more efficient than small local heaters (radiant heaters, fan heaters, electric radiators), but they often end up costing you more because you heat rooms that you aren't using.

With central forced-air heating, the furnace should be as close to the center of the house as possible so that the air ducts are short and no heat is wasted. In the worst possible case, where the heater is located beside an exterior wall, you can waste a lot of money heating the atmosphere outside the house.

4.4   GAS

Gas is a wonderful heating medium: economical, controllable, and not subject to the whims of oil producers. Gas stoves are also the most controllable medium for cooking: most professional chefs insist on gas burners (though they may prefer electric ovens).

The main drawback to gas is that if it escapes, it can blow the house to bits. It is advisable, therefore, to check *all* gas connections carefully, and if you smell leaking gas, not to go looking for the leak with a lighted match or with a cigarette in your mouth!

Most people who have had gas heating will place this high on their list of priorities when looking for a new house; it *really is* that good.

Main Supply

Mains gas is far and way the best option, if you can get it, and there is really very little to check. The technology is well understood — it has been around for almost a century-and-a-half — and safety standards are rigorous: gas companies are always very willing to check potential problems, and they take excellent care of their mains distribution. In long-established cities where the mains are *very* old, there may be occasional problems, but this is very rare.

Usually, if gas is available in an area, it will be piped into all the houses in that area — which is just as well, because paying for a "hook-up" in a house that is not supplied is likely to cost more than $1000, maybe several times more.

In older houses, though, there may sometimes be an "invisible" gas supply. If a previous owner decided to switch to electricity, usually because it was more "modern," the gas supply may have been capped while still remaining sound. In this case, restoring the gas supply should not cost much at all.

Bottled Gas

Bottled gas is useful for cooking and for local heating, but few private houses have the very large storage tanks that are needed for bottled-gas central heating. If the owner of the house that you are looking at is using much bottled gas, you should ask yourself whether you want to continue to do the same, or whether you might find electricity more convenient.

Gas Systems

Gas water heaters have already been mentioned, and gas clothes dryers are sometimes encountered. Check the vents on clothes dryers; make sure that the vent is not crushed, and that the gas line is not kinked. Remember, too, that a gas clothes dryer is a part-gas, part-electric appliance, so inspect it from the point of view of both systems. Like other appliances, it's no big deal unless the seller makes it so.

Gas-fired central heating is normally of two kinds. One is a gas-fired boiler which circulates hot water through radiators, and the other is the "heat exchanger" type. Circulatory heating systems are covered below in a later section, so heat-exchanger systems are all that is covered here.

Remove the front cover from the furnace and make sure that no part of the heat exchanger is cracked or damaged; if it is, dangerous "hot spots" can develop, and the furnace should be turned off immediately. Check that the flames are centered in each bank of heat-exchanger elements; again, "hot spots" can develop if they are not. *Any* "hot spots" are bad news, whether you can see a reason for them or not; if there is no obvious reason, the air-flow across the heat exchanger is probably uneven. No matter what the fault, "hot spots" mean that a heating engineer should be called in before the heater is run again.

As with any gas appliance, check the flue carefully to make sure that all products of combustion are being funnelled safely to the outside. As already mentioned, carbon dioxide is dangerous (it can suffocate you), but carbon monoxide (another combustion product) is poisonous and can be fatal.

Time for Another Apology

At the beginning of this chapter, I told you that you had taken care of the difficult stuff with the interior and exterior inspections — and now I'm telling you that badly-installed or badly-maintained gas appliances can kill you!

Once again, I must emphasize two things. The first is that these faults are *not common*: usually, everything is in good working order. The other point is that these faults are usually pretty easy to spot — and wouldn't you rather know how to spot them, so that you can either reject the house or have the faults put right, rather than finding about the dangers (and about the problems) *after* you had bought the house? Or even after you had paid a building inspector $200 to tell you things that you could have learned for yourself with the help of this book?

4.5   OTHER SYSTEMS

Years ago, I developed a theory that the cost of living has *never* really gone up. If you were prepared to live in the same conditions as your stone-age ancestors, in a cave or mud hut, dressed only in a few animal skins or home-woven cloth, and eating wild fruit and vegetables and the occasional small animal that you could knock on the head, it would not cost you much. It wouldn't be much fun, either — which is one of the reasons that we make our lives more complicated by adding things like telephones, security systems, cable television and so forth.

Telephone

There's not much to check here: either you have phone service or you don't. You may, however, want to check how many rooms have phone outlets, and how many lines are available — or even if you can have a private line at all (some areas still require a party line). Most people only want one line, but if you work at home, or if you live (for example) with elderly parents, you may well want an extra line. Find out what it would cost to get it installed.

Television and Cable Television

If you are used to watching particular shows or a particular channel that you don't want to do without, make sure that you can pick up the programs you want in the area that you are looking at. Often, small local variations even between houses can mean a very much better signal, or a very much worse one. Checking is easy enough: you just ask the seller to turn on his television, and check the channels available. Checking TV channels may not be in the same league as looking for settled foundations or decaying roofs, but if it is an important item to your way of living, you should take it into account when you are considering a house.

Check the TV aerial, too. Sometimes these are so badly installed as to be dangerous: they could literally fall (or be blown) off the roof. Of course, if the house has cable service, there probably won't be an aerial antenna.

Most modern houses are automatically wired for cable television when they are built; the service you receive for your "connection fee" amounts to little more than the company throwing a switch and giving you a decoder. Even with a house that is not prewired, the connection fee will not be high: the cable TV people are going to make their money on your monthly fees. As with broadcast television, though, not all cable services are available in all areas. If this is important to your family, check with the local cable company.

Security Systems

If any kind of security system is installed, check the following points:

Alarm — Is it local only, or is it hooked up to a local company who, in turn, alerts the police when your alarm goes off?

False Alarms — Is there a history of false alarms? If so, neighbors may disregard the system — or they may regard it as a nuisance rather than as a security system. Is there any kind of call-out fee for false alarms? If so, how much?

Sensors — How is the system triggered? Pressure pads? Switches on the windows? Door sensors, which go off when the door is opened? Light beams? Heat sensors?

Arming and Disarming — How do you turn the system on and off? If you buy this house, you don't want to set off the alarm system accidentally. It would be understandable if the owner did not want to tell you too much about the alarm system *before* he sells you the house, but he had better bet able to tell you all about it *afterwards!*

Smoke Detectors and Fire Control

It is a good idea to have at least one smoke detector in the house, and two or three are not too many. Do they work? Many people remove the battery because they get tired of false alarms: I have to open the windows and turn on the extractor fan in the kitchen when I "flame" food in brandy, or our smoke alarm goes off!

Don't put a smoke detector in the kitchen, but *do* consider hallways, basements and garages — the last two are often overlooked because they are not "living space."

Many smoke alarms show that they are "armed" with an intermittently flashing light — or you can test them with the aid of a cigar (or a flamed steak!). "Mains" smoke alarms have the advantage that you don't have to replace batteries, but if the power goes out, so does the alarm. This is not much use if the fire is the result of an electrical fault. To remember to replace batteries, choose a specific day each year, and think of it as giving the house a present: a "birthday present" if you choose your birthday as the day, or a "Christmas present" or even a "Thanksgiving present" as part of the thanks for another safe year.

Dispose of old or broken smoke detectors carefully: do not crush them. Many of them function by monitoring the decay of a tiny speck of high radioactive material. The speck is completely harmless *unless* you managed to swallow it (it could stick to a finger if you broke the alarm up) or breathe it in. Strictly, you should hand it over to a low-level hazardous waste disposal facility.

Fire control sprinklers are a double-edged sword: one false alarm can ruin a lot of furnishings, electronics, carpets and more. If you do have fire control sprinklers, "fusible link" types that are triggered by heat are *much* safer than the sort that is electronically controlled, though they do not kick in until the fire is rather better established.

Look at least for a fire extinguisher in the kitchen, and if the owner takes it with him, replace it when you move in. Make sure that the pressure indicator is good, and get the extinguisher recharged if need be.

4.6   INSULATION AND HEATING

As I have said elsewhere in this book, the importance of insulation and heating will depend to a very great extent on where you live: in central California, where I live, it is not as great a problem as it was in, say, upstate New York where my wife was born.

Also, of all the things that existing homeowners lie about, heating bills are one of the most fruitful fields for misinformation. Partly, of course, this may come down to different standards: if I like a room at 75° and you like it at 85°, while she likes it at 65°, our expectations are as different as our heating bills! Don't be afraid to ask to see gas or electricity bills.

One point that is worth making is that the traditional open fire may look very welcoming, but it is an unbelievably inefficient way to heat a room. Most of the heat goes straight up the chimney (though a few houses have surprisingly sophisticated heat exchangers and back boilers to recapture this heat), and if you merely want to have a fire as a supplement to central heating, you should be aware that you will almost certainly get what the professionals call a "negative heat benefit."

If you think hard about a "negative benefit," you will soon realize the unpleasant truth about what they are saying, which is this: if you put in a fire, you will actually lose more heat than you gain by burning the fuel! I am not joking about the terminology: that is *exactly* what a "fireplace consultant" told me when I considered reopening a fireplace in my centrally-heated house.

Insulation

Because attic insulation is so widely touted as a means of increasing the energy efficiency of a house, it is easy to forget that heat will escape *anywhere* it gets the chance — not just upwards!

For example, a wall that is shared with an unheated garage is a potential route for heat to escape, and so is a floor that spans an unheated cellar. In both cases, insulation is highly desirable.

Insulation normally comes on a roll, with a plastic vapor barrier on one side; that vapor barrier should face the *warm* side (the room) rather than the cold side (the cellar or the garage), because otherwise you are inviting condensation inside the insulation. This not only reduces the insulating effect of the materials (by a fairly small amount); it also gives the potential for fungus attack and for all the other woes that are attendant upon letting water remain in contact with timber. If there are multiple layers of insulation, there should only be *one* vapor barrier, for the same reason. It may look neat and tidy to have two layers, with the vapor barrier facing outwards on both sides, but it is not a good idea.

In many older houses, there is no wall cavity insulation. If you want to tear the walls down, you can install regular roll-type installation, but fortunately there is an easier way: several companies offer insulation systems which involve drilling holes at intervals, then blowing or pumping insulation in between the inner and outer walls. Because balloon-frame houses do not normally have fire-stops between floors, unlike platform-frame houses, they are much easier to insulate in this way: a platform-frame house requires more holes.

Needless to say, this sort of insulation must be competently installed, and the holes through which the insulation is blown *must* be carefully sealed, or the damage done by water ingress through the holes will far outweigh the benefits of insulation. If you see holes that might be evidence of this sort of insulation, ask the owner when it was done, the name of the company that did it, what sort of insulation it is, and whether it is fire-rated.

Finally, do not get too obsessed with insulation. We have all been in houses or (more usually) hotels where there was an unpleasant "hermetically sealed" feeling to the rooms. A house has to be able to "breathe" slightly, or it will become stuffy and may even cause allergies.

Central Heating — Fuels

I have already discussed the relative merits of electric and gas heating. Oil burners are subject to much the same observations as for gas burners — in particular, check the condition of the flue — but you might also care to ask the age of the oil-burner "gun" (the sprayer). Modern guns are much more efficient than old ones.

In fact *any* modern furnace is likely to be more efficient than an old one, and this is especially true where an old solid-fuel (usually coal) furnace has been converted to oil burning. A modern furnace is likely to give anything from forty percent to eight percent more heat for each dollar that you spend on fuel than you would get from an older furnace. Modern furnaces are much more compact, too.

It is unlikely that you will encounter any houses which still use an old-fashioned solid-fuel boiler, but it may happened. While solid-fuel furnaces are not as inconvenient as you may imagine, they are not particularly convenient; as a rule, it is a good idea to replace them.

You may, however, find a modern wood-burning stove, and you may be surprised at how efficient these things are. Not all of them provide hot water, but some do, and they are certainly ecologically sound.

Even more ecologically sound is solar heating: this is normally done by circulating water through black-painted panels on the roof top which raises the water to something around blood heat even on quite cool days; the extra heat required to get the water pipe hot then comes from some other source (electricity, gas, wood-fired stove, etc.). The only trouble is that many solar heating panels may have been installed by those whose ecological enthusiasm was greater than their skill at plumbing. If this is the case, the water can be contaminated in half a dozen ways, with rust and bacteria and (once again) corrosion residue and undetermined detritus (crud). Always have solar heating checked out professionally.

If there is any kind of boiler, always ask the owner of the house to put it on within a few minutes of your arrival, even if it is a warm summer's day. You want to be sure that it actually works; that heat comes out of all the places that it is supposed to come out of; and that there are no leaks anywhere in the system. When you turn it off, check *both* cut-off switches, the regular one and the emergency or backup switch.

While the boiler is operating, look for water or water stains on the floor beside it, which may well indicate a leak or crack, and check the outside (which will be hot!) for corrosion.

All boilers will last longer and work better if they are flushed and cleaned periodically. This may be done annually, or every couple of years; or if the water in the area is unusually soft and pure, it can be safely be stretched to a three- or even five-year period. Ask the house owner when the boiler was last cleaned and flushed — don't ask him when it was "serviced," or he may just tell you when it was last repaired!

Steam Heating

The steam-heating system was exactly what it said: steam was discharged from the boiler, under a modest pressure, and ran all through the various radiators, cooling steadily as it did so, until it finally condensed and was fed back into the boiler.

Although it was admirably simple, it had its drawbacks. One was that it was very hard to control: radiators near the furnace were often blisteringly hot, while those toward the limits of its travel might never rise about tepid. Another was that all the fittings were big, heavy, and expensive. A third, which is more alarming in theory than in practice, is that steam leaks are more dangerous (though generally less damaging to the fabric of the house) than hot-water leaks.

You may still find some steam-heating systems today, but they are dying out; you will probably do better to replace them with a hot-water system (see below).

Hot Water Heating

The hot-water system, where the boiler heats water that is circulated through radiators by a complicated set of pipes, is probably the most efficient and controllable form of central heating. The water circulates through narrow-bore copper pipes, and the heat given off by an individual radiator can be controlled by opening or closing the valve. The whole system operates at a very modest pressure and is extremely reliable.

The only drawback to the hot water system is its price: it is considerably more expensive at the construction stage than ducted-air heating.

At the highest radiator in the house, you may find that air very slowly accumulates in the system and has to be "bled" every now and then — usually once or twice a year. You can spot the problem by feeling the radiator: if it is hot up to a certain level, then cold (or at least much cooler) above that, the water level is what divides the hot area from the cool area.

Bleeding is easy enough: you use a small key and CAREFULLY "crack" the bleed valve at the top of the radiator. Some people who have lived with central heating for years do not know that you can do this, or are afraid to do it because they think it is too difficult.

Radiant-Floor Heating

Hot water is sometimes used for "radiant floor" heating, in which the "radiator" pipes are embedded in concrete or sandwiched between the sub-floor and a finished wood floor over the top.

This is not a particularly good system, because if it *does* go wrong, you are into major surgery and high-ticket bills when it comes to repairs. Although it is inherently a reliable system if it is properly installed, nothing lasts forever.

It also tends to have a slow response time (it takes while to heat up the floor and then to let it cool again), and it may not work all that well with a modern boiler, which usually relies on circulating larger volumes of relatively cooler water when compared with older boilers: 80° to 100°, instead of 120° to 140°.

Ducted-Air Heating

Ducted air heating is not particularly efficient, nor is it nearly as controllable as hot-water heating, but it does have three big advantages.

The first is that it is probably the cheapest possible system to install in a new building, which endears it to house builders.

The second is that warm air is totally non-threatening stuff, at least when compared with steam or circulating hot water. You don't have to worry about leaks and damage.

The third is that the same ducts that are used for heating in winter can also be used for central air conditioning in summer.

Because of these advantages, ducted-air heating is increasingly common. I described in an earlier section how to examine a *gas*-fired heat exchanger. Electrical "furnaces" cannot really be examined by a layman — or rather, you will not learn much if you try.

4.7   AIR CONDITIONING

Central air conditioning, like central heating, is one of those little luxuries which should theoretically be more efficient than running several separate air conditioners, but which usually ends up costing you more because you leave the air-conditioning on in rooms which you would not otherwise air-condition.

All air conditioners draw a tremendous amount of power, and central air conditioners have particularly dramatic power requirements: 4000 watts (4 Kw) is by no means unusual, and units of 5000 watts or more are quite common. The voltage "surge" effects of a big air conditioner kicking in and out can have terrible effects on electronic appliances and, indeed, you have probably been in many places where the lights dim temporarily as the air conditioner switches on.

Normally, therefore, central air conditioners have their own separate power supply, with an isolator switch. The air conditioner name plate will describe the kind of power supply it requires (for example, 5-amp fused junction box), and in order to comply with the electrical code, it must be connected to *exactly* that kind of junction box: if it calls for a fused box, a circuit breaker box *will not do*.

Check the condition of the evaporator and condenser coils: the evaporator coil (which does the cooling) will be near the central heating boiler, at the middle of the ducted-air system, while the condenser coil (which sheds the heat it has gathered from inside the house) will be outside, often sitting on top of the compressor.

If you can, you should ascertain the age of the unit: warranties are usually for seven years, but may only be for five or may be for as much as ten. This gives you a good idea of how long the manufacturers expect the unit to last, though there are units which are a quarter of a century old, or more, and are still working well.

4.8   HEAT PUMPS

Heat pumps have been touted for some time as the wave of the future. The theory is (fairly) simple. On cold days, they take heat from the outside environment and pump it into the inside of the house. On hot days, they take heat out of the inside of the house and dump it in the surroundings. They can, therefore, act both as heater and as air conditioners.

Unfortunately, the technology is not as simple as the theory. Heat pumps are expensive to install, and at the time of this writing, it was doubtful whether it was possible to recover the initial cost of the unit over the actual lifetime of the unit: in other words, it might just be easier and cheaper to stick with conventional methods of heating and cooling, at least for a few years yet.

5.0   __THE GREAT OUTDOORS__

Sunbathing ... inviting a few friends around for a barbecue ... somewhere secure for the kids to play ... for the dog to run ... a lawn, and some well-tended flowers. Well, maybe you can't have all these at once (dogs and kids can play havoc with flower gardens!), but they are all a part of the attraction of a yard.

Before you get too carried away about the yard, though, ask yourself if those dreams are *really* your dreams, or whether they just sound good. For many people, a yard is one of the greatest pleasures of owning a house, but for some, it's just waste land.

Do you sunbathe? Fewer and fewer people do, today. Even if they have the time, they're worried about skin cancer. Do you actually *like* barbecues? I know that they are as American as apple pie, but some people don't like apple pie, either (actually, I like barbecues, but I don't like apple pie). Do you have kids and a dog? And are you willing to mow laws, weed flowerbeds, and generally put in the effort that it takes to run a garden? I don't want to cry "bah! Humbug!" but quite honestly (with the exception of the barbecue), I'd be as happy in a downtown apartment with no yard as I would be in a house with a small yard; and I really would not want a big garden, just because it is so much work. You may well be different — but it's still a good idea to examine *your* desires and *your* preferences, rather than just going along with the crowd (or the real estate agent).

Much the same applies to those other symbols of the American outdoor life. Porches, stoops, patio and decks — and sunrooms and verandas, for that matter — are all a way of blurring the distinction between indoor and outdoor life, and very enjoyable they can be; but you had better be reasonably sure that you are going to use them, because otherwise, they are just that much more that has to be maintained. Personally, I love them — but you may not.

Finally, swimming pools are something to approach with caution. Once again, the dream is great: a cool relaxing drink, a cool relaxing swim, lounging around with some friends. The down side, though, is keeping the pool free of algae, leaves, and other trash, keeping the water pure and clean, repairing leaks in the pool and/or water lines, and always worrying in case a child falls in and drowns. For me, the balance tips against a pool, but once again, you may feel completely differently. Let's look at each of the outdoor features of a house in turn:

5.1   YARDS

The first thing to do with the yard is to find out who owns it. Quite often, the ownership of some parts of the yard is disputable. For example, there are those sidewalks that are separated from the road by a few feet of grass. Is that yours? Or is it the responsibility of the city parks department? Ownership has its responsibilities as well as its privileges: if you own it, you can treat it as an extension of your garden, but you might also beheld liable if someone tripped over a tree-stump and broke a leg. If it belongs to the city parks department, they may or may not mind if you plant flowers, but you had better check before you do so.

Likewise, with older houses, it is by no means unusual for there to be a picket fence (or even a stone wall) set well within the actual property boundary — anything from a couple of feet to a couple of yards. In more relaxed times, this was often a showcase for a riot of flowers: now, you may be lucky if it is not used at all and sundry as a parking space. If it is a part of the public highway, you cannot stop people parking there, but if it is a part of your property, you can post NO PARKING signs or even move the fence.

Sometimes there are even areas which it seems that *no one* owns. My father-in-law's house is an excellent example. It is built on the edge of a low mesa, which slopes down for six or seven feet to pasture land. When he bought the house, it had a boundary fence which was about 20 feet from the pasture-land fence. He has been trying for three years to find out who owns the land in between. The former landowner, from whose farmland the housing lots were carved out, denies that it is his; his land, he says, starts at the pasture fence. The city denies that it is theirs. If it *does* belong to my father-in-law, he plans to fence it before a child is hurt playing there.

Landscaping

"Landscaping" is a somewhat grandiose name for what most of us call "gardening"; it is the layout of the lawns, shrubs, flowerbeds and so forth. Maybe it's "gardening" when you do it, and "landscaping" when you pay someone else to do it!

Although you might think that landscaping is one of the easiest things in the world to change, in practice it can be time-consuming or expensive or (quite often) both, even for quite simple changes. For example, it is not that difficult to fill in a flower-bed with sod, but if you do not pack the earth down well before you lay the turfs, you will soon find that your lawn has a disconcerting hollow in the middle of it, where the new part has sunk. The only way to deal with this is to dig it up and put in some more earth. Or, again, you decide that the ornamental wall which the previous owner built out of bottles is hideous and has to go. Once you attack it, you find that it is built like Fort Knox and that archaeologists ten thousand years in the future will be puzzling over it long after your house has crumbled to dust.

The things to look out for, then are these:

Aesthetics — If you really can't stand the landscaping, but you want to buy the house, it is going to cost a fair amount of time or money or both if you want to change it.

Dangerous Layouts — These can be personal dangers (ugly little fountains at shin level that are easy to fall over), or dangers to the house (a nearby bank set up against the house, just inviting moisture damage to the structure of your investment).

Realistic Layouts — A really beautiful garden requires a great deal of upkeep. Unless you have the time and inclination to do this yourself, or unless you can hire someone to do it for you, you had better set your sights on a more realistic target — more lawn, perhaps, and fewer annual plants that require constant replanting and weeding. If the present owner of the house is retired, the garden may be his or her main occupation in life; whereas if you have to earn a living, you could not hope to maintain that standard. Of course, if you are the one that is retired, or about to retire, and you have always longed for a garden like this, it could be perfect for you.

Insurability — Dangerous paths may void your homeowner's liability insurance (this is usually provided free with contents insurance or other insurances). Dangerous trees may mean that you can't claim if (say) a branch falls through your roof. Your yard *must*, therefore, be reasonably safe.

Trees

Let's take it for granted that threes and shrubs are attractive to look at, provide welcome shade, and so forth: we all know their advantages. As so often in this book, we have to look behind the immediate, romantic aspect and make cold, hard judgments of potential problems.

One word of warning, though. Don't get carried away when looking at the potential hazards of trees. The dangers are mostly slight and avoidable. If you cut down every tree in sight, you would probably have a safer environment. But would you still want to live there?

Unsound Trees — A tall tree can weigh several thousand pounds. When it gets old, it can fall over. Put these two factors together — and put your house in the way when the tree *does* fall over — and you can see the potential problems.

Some trees are very much more dangerous than others: elms, for example, are particularly treacherous. If the house that you are looking at is anywhere near the possible path of a falling tree, you would be well advised to have the trees examined by a professional tree surgeon.

Unsound Branches — Even if the trees are sound, they can always lose branches. Again, take a tree surgeon's advice on which branches (if any) need to be trimmed or removed.

Branches Brushing or Close to the Roof — Even if the branches are perfectly sound, they should not be too close to the roof of the house. If they are actually touching the roof, they could damage the roof, they could damage the roof covering. If they are merely close to the roof, they will slow down the drying of the roof after a heavy rain. If the roofing is perfectly sound, this should not matter, but as a matter of principle, it is always as well to keep moisture to a minimum.

Dead Wood — Dead wood, whether standing or cut, is a favorite refuge for termites. DO NOT burn termite-infested wood inside the house, for obvious reasons; ideally, have it removed, or burn it in a bonfire a good distance from the house (but first check with local authorities about the legality of burning in your yard!). If there is evidence of termite investigation in dead wood, pay special attention to a possible termite attack in the house; you may even wish to have the house treated for termites, whether you can see the termites in the house or not, in order to get an anti-termite guarantee from the exterminators. It will be a lot less hassle to have the exterminators in *before* you move in, rather than afterwards. In many states, a termite inspection is a requirement before the bank will even lend you the money to buy a home, so <u>there will be little chance that this problem would be a surprise to you.</u>

Root Damage — Large trees or shrubs can, if they are planted too close to the house, send out roots which can damage foundations, either directly (they can worm their way into the smallest crack) or indirectly, by opening up channels through which water can seep into the foundations.

Although it is by no means an infallible rule, it is generally fair to assume that the roots of a tree spread out about as far as its branches.

Fast-Growing Varieties — I knew someone once who decided that he wanted a screen of trees between the end of his garden and the road. He sent for some fast-growing trees (I think they were *Cupressus magnus*).

When they arrived, he could not believe what puny little things they were, but he planted them anyway. "It was like Jack and the Beanstalk," he says. They are now monsters, far bigger than he wanted, and he has to keep trimming them to hold them in check. If there are small, recently planted trees in the yard of the house you are inspecting, be aware that this can happen.

Driveways and Paths

When you inspect the various kinds of walkway or driveway that can exist in a yard, you are checking for four things: appearance, utility, possible dangers, and blocked access to drains, etc. Replacing a driveway can cost literally thousands of dollars, while replacing even a modest concrete path can cost many hundreds, so check them carefully! With *all* paths and driveways, look out for "heaves" caused by tree roots. These are not going to get any better, and if the root is still alive, there is a very good chance that they will get worse.

Appearance — Cracked or eroded blacktop or concrete is rarely a problem for an automobile, either to drive over or to park on, but it looks terrible. Concrete is sometimes repairable, if the damage is not too bad, but the patchwork effect that you get when you repair it is rarely attractive.

Blacktop is easier to repair, provided the damage is not too bad: you can even buy patching kits in hardware stores, and you can also buy a sealer which would be applied annually to make sure that the blacktop remains in good condition. If the surface has deteriorated too badly, though, you are back into a complete replacement and a stiff bill.

Utility — Put bluntly, a path should make it easier for you to get where you want to go. If a path does not lead anywhere, or if it is one of those ankle-breaking "stepping stone" paths where the stones are not properly sunk into the surrounding earth, it is not much of a path. I have seen houses where I would sooner rip up the path than try to use it!

Possible Danger — This is closely related to my last point. If there is any possibility that anyone could trip or hurt themselves because of a dangerously uneven path, GET THE PATH FIXED if you buy the house. You only need one delivery man or paper boy or casual caller to trip and break an arm or leg, and you will probably hear from the lawyers.

Of course, the meaning of "dangerously uneven" is open to interpretation. Even one of those stepping-stone paths that I referred to as an ankle-breaker may not lay you open to a lawsuit, but a path that is *supposed* to be flat and smooth and even, and is not, is another matter. In particular, this applies to concrete or flagstones that have been "heaved" by tree roots or (more rarely) by frost damage. Again I say, GET THEM FIXED if you buy the house — and be aware that getting more than a very few square yards of path fixed may well prove to be hazardous to your wealth!

Blocked Access to Drains — This is one that I would not have thought of if it had not happened to me. In the first house I bought, there should have been a manhole cover right in the middle of the back yard, where you could gain access to the main drain. Instead, there was a concrete path over the top. The professional building inspector whom I had hired — this was before I learned to do things for myself — advised me of this, and said that if anything did go wrong with the drains, the path would have to be torn up.

I asked his advice, and he said, "If I were you, I'd just hope that nothing goes wrong with the drains. It's a fairly new house, so they shouldn't have any problems. And if it does have to come up — well, it's only a yard wide; I'd re-cover it with flagstones instead of concrete.

Nothing ever did go wrong, either — an excellent illustration of what I have tried to stress all through the book — that mostly, things *don't* go wrong: and especially they won't go wrong if you are on the lookout for problems. I've forgotten who said it, but for a long time, one of my favorite sayings has been, "Fortune favors the prepared mind."

Steps

A broken step is almost a by-word for something dangerous that you could trip on, so check any steps with special care. Check the treads (the horizontal parts) first. If they are badly damaged, it is going to be expensive to replace them — and that is only if they are made of concrete or cement-faced brick. If they are made of stone, it is going to be *very* expensive to replace them. Replacing wood steps is cheaper, but wood is not really the best material: you might do better to consider replacements in brick.

Next, check the risers (the vertical parts). Broken risers weaken the steps and look awful. Once again, replacement is expensive.

Third, check the side walls. In particular, are they vertical? If they are out of alignment, they will have to be replaced and, yes, you've guessed it; it's an expensive job.

Finally, check the hand rail. Try to rock it; is it solidly fixed? Mercifully, this is not usually a very expensive thing to repair. If there is no hand-rail, you (or may not) decide that you need to add one.

Retaining Walls

When I was in my teens, my girlfriend lived in an absolutely beautiful house that was about 150 years old. It was huge, and built of granite; and because a new road had been built past it, the front garden was restrained by a retaining wall some 12 feet high. Whenever I went to see her, I skirted that wall carefully: once, in the 1930s, it had burst and killed two people.

Anywhere that houses are built on hills, there are likely to be retaining walls that are holding back hundreds of tons of dirt. As long as these walls are only a few feet high — preferably only three or four feet, and certainly not more than five or six feet — there is very little to worry about. In some places, though, retaining walls are ten or fifteen or even twenty feet high. Like any other wall, these walls can age, or they can be weakened by tree roots. If they fail, the results can be disastrous.

You should, therefore, think very hard indeed before you even consider the purchase of a property with a very high retaining wall around the garden, even if it is offered at a bargain price. After all, the reason for the bargain price may be that the seller is worried about the retaining wall!

If you are prepared to take the risk then you should obviously check the condition of the retaining wall very carefully indeed, looking at the mortar and the overall condition of the masonry, and looking for any tell-tale bulges in the wall which could be omens of impending trouble. Of course, you will ask your professional building inspector for his opinion, but do not be surprised if he leaves himself an escape route in his written report: something like, "although [the wall] appears to be sound, it is impossible to guarantee its structural integrity without major excavations." The risks he is trying to cover himself (and you) against are these:

Personal Injury — If anyone is standing close to the wall when it fails, hey may be seriously injured or even killed. Quite apart from the moral implications, this is once again an open invitation to the legal profession.

What's more, it is often a question not of *whether* you are liable, but of how much it is going to cost you. In many areas, failing (or falling) masonry is a matter of "strict liability." In other words, you will be held responsible, no matter what happens. There is no way that you can prove that you took "all reasonable precautions," because the doctrine of strict liability expressly rules out the possibility.

Damage to the Building — When the wall at Elm Villa (my girlfriend's house) went, it was far enough from the house that there was no damage to the structure of the main building; it was just a question of rebuilding the wall. In some places, though a collapsed retaining wall can lead to major earthslides which can even leave part of the foundations exposed.

Unbelievable Expense — The cost of rebuilding a major retaining wall that collapses onto a public highway can run into the tens of thousands of dollars. What is more, it may be disputable who has to pay for it — you, or the highway authority. They are unlikely to volunteer to pay, but they are very likely to put considerable pressure on you to have the wall fixed. In one city where I lived, a 25-foot-high retaining wall collapsed for something like thirty yards, and the owner of the house bounded by the wall said that he would declare bankruptcy if he had to pay: the cost was estimated at $150,000 to $200,000. I don't know what happened: when I left the city two years later, the matter was still unresolved, though I believe that the highway authority had agreed to pay some or all of the rebuilding cost.

Rights of Way and Other Legal Considerations

There are all kinds of invisible, *legal* features which may affect your enjoyment of the property. Although they are not visible, it is still possible to check them by asking the property owner about them, and by checking the title carefully (this will be done along with the title search). Below I have given three of the most important features of this kind: you will see how they can be relevant when you are inspecting and how certain conditions or situations — crossing someone else's land, for example — should alert you to the necessity of checking them out.

Rights of Way — A right of way is exactly what its name suggests, the right to pass over a given piece of land, but without any ownership.

Obviously a right of way may work to your advantage, or to your disadvantage. If the public has a right of way across your property, you cannot stop their free movement — for example, by building a wall. If you have a right to cross someone else's property, then equally, they are not allowed to stop you.

Rights of way are usually time-savers — short cuts — there are times when the only access to a piece of property may be a right of way across another piece of property. Rights of way may be specifically granted (in which case there is very little you can do about them) or they may be acquired.

Acquiring a right of way normally requires that the way should be used regularly or often, and that it should be used "*nec vi, nec clam, nec precario*" — in other words, "not by force, nor secretly, nor by permission." In addition, it must be used for some time, typically anything from five or seven years to about twenty years (this varies from jurisdiction to jurisdiction).

If the seller of a house says, "There is a right of way across here," but nothing appears on the title search, it is a good idea to have an attorney check it out to see whether there really is nor not. If, after you buy the house, you want to make sure that a right of way is *not* created, all you have to do is put up a sign which says something like, "this is private property and permission to pass over it is revocable at any time. It has not been dedicated and will not be dedicated as a right of way." That way, anyone who uses the short cut is doing so "precario" — by permission — and you are not losing your proprietary rights.

Ancient Lights — In *some* jurisdictions, windows that have been in place for more than a certain length of time (typically twenty or thirty years) are legally "ancient lights," and the owner of the property is entitled to stop anyone else building in such a way that it would significantly cut down on the amount of light coming through the window. If you own the ancient lights, you can stop other people building. If the other person owns them, they can stop you from building.

Easements — An easement is the legal right to make limited use of someone else's property. For example, you might have the right to cross your neighbor's land in order to park your car. But the easement is effectively a private arrangement between two landowners: just because one person has an easement permitting him to cross another's land, it does not mean there is a public right of way.

Historically, there were all kinds of easements, such as the right to use water from a stream which was on someone else's property, or even the right to collect firewood from his woods, but private easements are less and less common in the United States; the most interesting ones are mostly Old World hangovers from feudal times. More common are easements granted to public utility companies to do work on electric and gas lines, and to come onto your property to read your meters for billing purposes.

5.2   PORCHES, PATIOS AND DECKS

In the right environment, "jes' sett'n" is as enjoyable a way to relax as it was in our grandparents' or great-grandparents' day; and although the rocker on the stoop is no longer the classic image of America that it once was — air conditioning has, to a large extent, replaced cool, shady places — there are still plenty of towns and cities where the tradition survives unbroken to this day. Certainly, sitting on a "planter's chair" on a shady porch in the Old South, preferably with a mint julep in your hand, is a great way to unwind after the stresses of the day.

Patios and decks are a bit more modern: they smack of inviting people around, rather than just having them drop in, but the aim is still the same. What you want to do is to blur the distinction between "inside" and "outside," so that you enjoy the best features of both.

Finally, a glassed-in sun room can greatly extend the season when you can sit out, if you live in a cold climate; and even if it's not sunny, a sun room is often a good, quiet place to read a book on a rainy day, listening to the quiet splash of the rain and getting lost in a good novel. For my money, porches, stoops, patios, verandas, decks and all of the other things covered in this section are what lift a house above mere accommodation — a "machine for living" — and turn it into a pleasure.

Porches and Stoops

What you call these things will depend on where you come from. Where I come from, a porch is a small enclosure which is little wider than the door it surrounds, and it can be open or glassed-in; the word "stoop" is never heard; and the long-roofed and open-sided (or more rarely, glassed-in) space which is the no-man's land between indoors and outdoors is called a veranda. It's interesting to learn where these words come from: "porch" comes from the Latin *portica* via the French *porche*; "stoop" is from the Dutch *stoep*; and "veranda" comes form the Hindi *varanda*. A balcony, for what it's worth, is an open veranda and comes from the Italian *balcone*.

No matter what you call them, they need to be looked at carefully. Because their structural woodwork (or more rarely, wrought-iron work or masonry) is exposed to the elements, they can deteriorate quite badly. Look for rotten wood, especially at ground level and at all joints; for broken or rotten floorboards; for signs of insect infestation, again with particular attention to joints and corners; for rusted-through ironwork, whether ornamental or in the form of supporting brackets; and if you can get underneath, check to make sure that there are no plants growing there, because this encourages moisture damage, infestation by insects and vermin, and even fire. All you need to stop things growing is plastic patio liner with a coat of sand, though concrete would be better.

Check the roof, especially where it is joined to the main wall: there should be lead or zinc flashing, and (of course) the roof itself should be sound. This is one place where corrugated galvanized iron *is* quite popular for roofing, and the stuff can rust. It's not particularly expensive to buy, but actually refitting it can be very time consuming, mostly because of rusted-in bolts.

In some areas, particularly the more humid parts of the Old South, verandas may be screened with bug-screen. This may not look too beautiful, but before you decide to tear it down, leave the door open one night with the lights on and see how much insect life you attract. The person who put those screens up may have known what he or she was doing! A good compromise is to have the front porch open (because it looks good, and you can sit there on fine evenings, but to have the back porch screened (a great place for breakfasts).

Patios

A patio is no more than open, paved space that allows you to "spill out" from your living room, kitchen or den (or sometimes other rooms) into the open air. It can be made of concrete, of patio blocks or even of brick or stone. The normal means of construction is to compact the earth well; lay a specially-treated plastic liner, obtainable from hardware stores; put a bed of sand on top of that, typically a couple of inches deep; and then top the whole thing off with patio blocks, filling the gaps between the blocks with sand. The edge of the patio is enclosed in some way — often with cement — to stop the sand running out.

The main thing to look for in a patio is that it is solid and even. If it is made of patio blocks, you could probably relay the thing yourself in a single block-breaking long weekend, but if it is made of concrete and it is badly cracked, you are looking at some expense to get it re-poured. You do *not* want a blacktop patio: they absorb heat, then re-radiate it like a furnace. It is also possible, on very hot days, for some of the blacktop to stick to your shoes and track in on your floors or carpets.

Decks

A deck is essentially a raised wooden patio — or alternatively, you could think of it as a large, roofless veranda (or stoop or porch!). It has the advantage that it is cooler than a patio, and that the wood of which it is constructed is less likely to become baking hot.

The best woods for decks are redwood and western red cedar, both of which will weather in a very attractive way, though you should apply preservative to the wood to help keep cracking to a minimum if you live anywhere other than the "sun belt." The third choice for deck construction is pressure-treated, kiln-dried lumber, which is significantly cheaper than the other two woods but is not nearly as good-looking and which is much more prone to warping. The preservative is usually chromated copper arsenate (look for the "CCA" stamp on the lumber), and some of this wood is so insect-resistant that it is guaranteed by the makers for life.

Look for stainless or galvanized nails in the deck, because ordinary iron nails will rust and discolor the surrounding wood, and (as with a porch), don't let any vegetation grow underneath. The easiest thing to do is to use patio liner and patio blocks or other stones, but I once saw a space under a deck where the owner had laid out a miniature, formal Japanese raked-sand garden. It was *very* pretty!

Sun Rooms

While an open veranda is fine is some areas, there are others where the climate simply isn't up to it. The answer is either a glassed-in veranda or a purpose-built sun room.

Structurally, the sun room can either be similar to the rest of the house, only with more glass, or it can be built like a greenhouse, typically with a frame of light alloy. Either way, checking the quality of construction is easy, but there are two particular points that will repay closer examination.

One is that there is not *too much* glass. Glass walls are one thing: a glass roof is quite another. Not only will a glass roof cause it to get *very hot indeed* inside (this is the **real** "greenhouse effect"); it will also require constant care if you are not to find green algae growing on the roof. This is unsightly, smells slightly funny, and rather removes the point of the glass roof.

The other thing to look for is plenty of ventilation. Even on a cold, sunny day, the interior of a glass-walled room can rapidly grow very hot and stuffy. When I lived in Bermuda, we used to get around this by opening the numerous French windows which opened from the drawing room and dining room into the glassed-in veranda; the big, old limestone house was always cool. In a friends' house in this country, though, there were no French windows, just a door. Dave used to have to leave the windows open in almost all weathers, unless it was actually raining or snowing heavily.

If you keep many plants in your sun room, you will also have to watch out for condensation, which can be very heavy. Once again, the only answer is plenty of ventilation (or a heavy-duty dehumidifier with its own drain).

5.3   POOLS AND HOT TUBS

The first thing to check about a pool is that it was built with the necessary permits. Because a pool is "just a hole in the ground" instead of a structure that rises above it, many people just don't think of getting a building permit — and yet many localities require them.

Nor is a permit for the pool the only problem. Building codes may also specify the kind of electrical supply that may be brought to the pool (usually by underground cables with a ground-fault interrupter); the minimum dimensions of the walkway around the pool; and that the pool be lit, usually be specific types of lights. Depending on the neighborhood you live in, you may even be required to do any or all of the following: surround the pool with a fence; post signs giving the depth of water in the pool; and post a sign saying that there is no lifeguard on duty. Usually, too, there most be no overhead power lines within a set distance of the pool.

Pool Construction

Pools may be made of tile, concrete, or other materials — even fiberglass. Examine the pool liner for damage, just as you would any other structure: cracks not only let the water out of the pool, but also can cause trouble with waterlogged soil, soil movement, and (depending on the lay of the land) possible damage to the foundations of the house to which the pool is attached *and other houses*. The possibilities for liability are not pleasant to contemplate.

Remember also that the water inside a pool is *extremely* heavy. A cubic foot of water weighs 62.5 lbs, so a pool that is about ten feet by twelve feet by four to six feet deep (a very small pool) contains about fifteen **tons** of water. This should show you why pools are normally dug into the ground (rather than having retaining walls), and why they are not built too close to a sudden drop-off!

Water

The plumbing for the filtration system should have been installed by a licensed plumber, and the pump should have been installed by a licensed electrician. Unfortunately, because building a pool *looks* easy, and because there used to be many articles in the do-it-yourself magazines about how to build pools (such articles have all but vanished today), you cannot rely on everything having been done legally or even properly.

Do You Really Want a Pool?

Now you can see why I would regard a pool with distinctly mixed feelings: it can be quite an additional resonsibility. But if you want a pool anyway, insist upon the following:

1. You can satisfy yourself that the pool was built totally in compliance with all relevant regulations

2. The pool is structurally sound

Hot Tubs

Maybe I've been living in California too long, but I have to admit that I think hot tubs are a good idea. Sure, they don't give you the exercise that a pool does, but they certainly do make you feel good. If you're not into entertaining large numbers of people, you can even hold hot tub parties — a big tub will hold six or eight people.

You can even sit in a hot tub, out of doors, on a snow day; I've never tried it personally, but I've met several people who have, and they say that it's a wonderful experience — rather like a traditional sauna in Finland, where you are supposed to get all heated up in the sauna and then go roll around in the snow, or swim in freezing water, before you get back in.

At this point, though, we are beginning to veer off into the realms of fantasy; and as this is a strictly practical book, it is time to get on to the first Appendix, which is a brief survey of the legal side of things.

APPENDICES

APPENDIX 1

LEGAL AND FINANCIAL CONSIDERATIONS

If you have this book, you almost certainly have Broughton Hall's *HOW TO FIND A BARGAIN HOME*, which gives a great deal of information about finding houses at bargain prices and also about the best way to finance them. The only purpose of this Appendix is to summarize the steps that are needed in buying a home — and to furnish a reminder.

The reminder is this: YOU ARE IN THE DRIVER'S SEAT. You do not need to be intimidated by anyone: real estate agents, sellers or attorneys. *You* are the one who is putting up the money; *you* are the one who has the right to make the decisions. The various professionals you deal with are there for your benefit, and if they won't do what you tell them, ask why not. If they can't give a satisfactory answer, you are not the one who is in the wrong! They should be able to help you with any or all of the steps below; but you are the one who is in charge.

Sometimes you may take these steps in a different order: for example, some people still prefer not to arrange financing until *after* they have found the property they want. Indeed, there are some cases where particular types of financing are available only after the specific house has been approved. Even so, the main steps are these:

1. DETERMINE YOUR BUDGET

Only you can do this, but there are several things to remember. One is that a mortgage is a tax shelter, so you can probably afford *more* in mortgage payments than you can in rent. The second is that it is worth making a few sacrifices at first: the capital appreciation that your investment in a home will bring you can be *impressive*. If it means cutting down on trips, meals out, and so forth, remember that this is only temporary, while the return on the house is long-term. Finally, even if you are on an adjustable rate mortgage, after a few years your mortgage payments will still look very cheap indeed compared with the rent you would be paying for a comparable place.

On the down side, though, remember that variable-rate mortgages can go up as well as down. If you buy at a time when interest rates are high, you will be okay if they don't go higher still; but if you buy when interest rates are low, just ask the mortgage company what another (say) two percent on the lending rate would do to your monthly payments. You may be surprised. *Don't over-extend yourself*; take the advice of the loan company, and be totally open with them. They are there to help you: what they want is for you to be able make regular monthly payments, so they are unlikely to encourage you to take on more than you can afford.

1.2   ARRANGE FINANCING

This is covered in *HOW TO FIND A BARGAIN HOME*; the advantage of using that book, instead of just calling around to various banks and other loan institutions, is that you will also get a handle on grants, low-cost loans, and federal programs of various kinds that are available to everyone.

1.3   FIND THE PROPERTY YOU WANT AND CHECK IT OUT

This is the subject of this whole book, so I do not need to say much here! There are, however, a couple of points worth making. The first is a repetition of advice given elsewhere in this book, while the other is covered in much greater detail in *HOW TO FIND A BARGAIN HOME*.

Get the House Professionally Inspected

Even though you have been through every single step outlined in this book, and used all the checklists, it is simply a way to weed out the houses you might otherwise have thought were fine. Once you have found the house you really want, and if it passes *your* inspection, you should still pay a qualified professional inspector to go over the house; he may spot some things that you have missed, but more importantly, he should be able to put your mind at rest concerning points where you are not sure. Get the house professionally inspected *before* you make a binding offer, but remember that you can put conditions into an offer: "subject to inspection" or even "subject to financing."

Make an Offer

Once the inspection is completed to your satisfaction, tell the seller so; he or she will be pleased that you have moved one step closer to purchase. You can now make your offer. Because the offer is a legal contract, and because it will commit you to spending a lot of money if it is accepted, it is normal to have the offer written by a professional — either a real estate agent, or an attorney (this varies from state to state). Your offer may be accepted "as is," or there may be a counter-offer and a certain amount of dickering. Or, of course, your offer can be rejected.

Once the offer has been accepted, it is normal to pay a few hundred dollars in "earnest money" (to show that you are serious about wanting the property) and some other monies (exactly what you pay is something to be determined in the offer) into escrow. The escrow company will hold the money until all the details are sorted out, after which they will pass it on to the seller. If anything goes badly wrong, they will return it to you.

1.4   BUY TITLE INSURANCE

The seller (or his title search company) will make sure that the seller has a good title which he can sell to you, and they will insure themselves to cover any possibility that they make a mistake in the title search. It is a VERY GOOD idea to buy additional title insurance, because the seller's title insurance normally does not cover any undiscovered liens or encumbrances (see Glossary), and while you may buy a *good* title, you may not up with a *free and clear* title. Often, the buyer's title insurance is one of the things that the seller agrees to pay for — make this clear in your offer.

1.5   COMPLETE THE SALE

Completion or closing is when you finally take over the responsibility for the house — and when the pride of ownership really hits you!

This is the moment you have been waiting for, and this is what this book is about. I won't say "good luck," because if you have used this book and *HOW TO FIND A BARGAIN HOME,* you will have made your own luck, and it *will* be good. So I'll just say this: *Enjoy your house!*

APPENDIX 2

THE GREAT RADON SCARE

Radon is a colorless, invisible, radioactive gas which is a decay product of naturally-occurring radium (NOT *uranium*, which is what most books will tell you — though radium is, in turn, a decay product of uranium). It is heavier than air, so it can accumulate in any hole in the ground, including basements and cellars. It is also one of the most-hyped scare stories of the last twenty years.

Basically, if there is radon mixed with the air you breathe, it increases your risk of developing lung cancer. Like most of these scare stories, though, the amount of radon the average person is exposed to is negligible. There is a tiny, tiny amount of radon in *all* the air that we breathe, and it is not the result of man's carelessness with nuclear weapons or nuclear reactors, either: it is a by-product of the radium that is found in many types of rock. Because it is heavy, the radon concentration is always higher at ground level than at normal breathing height, and it can be even higher if you dig below ground level.

The vast majority of houses in the United States do not even have *detectable* amounts of radon in them (not without very sophisticated testing equipment, anyway), and in many cases where the radon levels are detectable, it is still disputable whether their effect is significant.

Assuming, though, that your house is built on pitchblende or carnotite (a yellowish impregnation of sandstone in the Western United States, a double vanadate of uranium and potassium), or that it is built of granite (which is remarkably radioactive stuff — New York's Grand Central Station is the most radioactive place in New York City!), you still don't have too much to worry about. As long as your cellar is well ventilated, the amount of radon that can build up is *still* unlikely to be significant.

About the only way that you could reliably build up a high enough radon concentration to do yourself any harm, at least in most of the United States, is to have a cellar with literally no ventilation, and to spend plenty of time down there. Most radon testing companies are preying on the frightened and the gullible, and most radon testing outfits are a waste of money, because they are used in three areas where there is no risk in the first place. If you are sincerely worried, call local environmental agencies: they will be able to tell you if there is even the possibility of a problem. They will also be able to recommend an *honest* radon testing company.

If you live in an area where radon concentrations are unusually high, you need to do your best to seal your cellar, crawl spaces and foundations against seepage of the gas (which is difficult) and to ventilate such areas well (which is easy).

Only if you live in a **very** radioactive area is there much chance of any problems arising in the house itself (as distinct from the cellar). All in all, radon is something that is well to be *aware* of, but it not something to *worry* about.

APPENDIX 3

PROPERTIES FOR PROFIT

Both this book and its companion, *HOW TO FIND A BARGAIN HOME*, are aimed mainly at the buyer who wants a single family home to live in. It is worth pointing out, though, that once you own one home, you have gained a great deal of experience which could be put to good use in buying another.

There are two ways that you might want to approach buying another house. One is to "trade up," moving into bigger and better houses in better parts of town, and the other simply to buy *more* property, either to sell at a profit or as a rental investment.

If you are "trading up," there is nothing much to add to what I have already said in the rest of the book: after all, you are looking out for a house for yourself, and what *you* want is what's important.

If, however, you are buying a house with the specific intention of making a profit, whether on the sale or by rental, there are two approaches you can take.

1.   "PLAYING SAFE"

For most rental or even resale purposes, you will do best to "play safe." Almost by definition, a "one in a million" house requires a tenant who is, if not "one in a million," at least a bit out of the ordinary. There are many more ordinary people out there than extraordinary ones; they are more predictable; and often, they're better payers, too. Maybe your fire engine-red converted lighthouse on the northern Washington coast would be perfect for some people (*I'd* be interested!), but there are going to be many more people who are interested in a four-room family apartment that's an easy commute from their jobs.

By the same token, don't make the decor too personal, and don't spend a fortune on super-deluxe features such as ultra high-quality carpet, lots of full-length mirrors in the bedrooms and bathrooms, fancy wallpaper, antique or bold-plated bathroom suites, jacuzzis, fancy landscaping and so froth, unless the house you are renting is also a deluxe house in a deluxe neighborhood. Most ordinary renters are not much affected by these things, so you are laying out a lot of money for no great increase in your return; indeed, if you are unlucky and get a bad tenant, an excess of luxury is easier to trash than a plain-vanilla house. If your tenants have good taste, on the other hand, they will use their personal possessions to enhance your basic decor — and they will appreciate neutral tones (beige, tan) against which they can set their own stuff. They may not be so keep on overpower decor, especially if it does not match their own taste.

2.   HIGHER STAKES

There is, however, another way of doing things — and it is diametrically opposed to the "play-it-safe" approach. It is to look for a property which as potential "down the road."

Often the place to look is just out of town, in areas that are almost certain to be the next areas for expansion. An unconsidered corner house, with a good bit of land, may barely pay for itself in rent for a year or two, and it may not earn a lot for four or five years. but when the city expands, and it's a prime site for a local market or even mini-mall, you are well to the good!

Likewise, think of a big house on one of the main roads just out of town — a road that is getting busier and busier, so that the attraction of the house *as a house* is decreasing. Now think of that big house converted into medical or legal offices ... Do you see the direction to take?

If you take this approach, instead of the "playing safe" approach, you will need to check zoning ordinances; look at the history of your town or city (because zoning ordinances change as the city expands); and satisfy yourself that (for example) the water and sewage supplies could handle the traffic that the conversion would engender. You will need to consider access for the disabled, and parking spaces, and more. All of this is far from the main thrust of this book — but I'm sure that you can use your own initiative, plus the information that *is* given in the main body of this book, to inspect the property with the conversion in mind.

GLOSSARY

NOTE: A word which is displayed in all capitals, such as BACKFILL or SOFFIT, is one that is defined in its appropriate (alphabetical order) place in this Glossary.

Abstract of Title

This is a summary of public records relating to the ownership of the land. Your attorney or title company or realtor will obtain and review these to make sure that there are no LIENS or other ENCUMBRANCES which could interfere with a "free and clear" TITLE to the land. If there are any problems, they will advance you on how to resolve them; if the problems cannot be resolved, they will advise you not to purchase the property.

Agreement of Sale

This is a CONTRACT which spells out exactly what the SELLER is selling and what the buyer is buying, and what the buyer is paying the seller. It is a good idea to have the Agreement of Sale examined by a lawyer specializing in these matters: for example, how would you feel if oil was found on "your" land, but you then found that the seller had retained the minerals rights, so the oil was his!

"Alligatoring"

This explains itself when you see it: a cracked paint finish like an alligator's hide. It is caused by paint drying unevenly on a badly-prepared surface, or by painting onto an undercoat that is not quite dry. In time, the paint will flake off. Even before it does, the protection it afford will not be adequate. See also BLISTERS.

Amp

Short for "ampere," a measure of electrical CURRENT. Because WATTS are equal to VOLTS x amps, you can work out the value needed for a fuse, or for a whole circuit. For example, a 120-volt appliance rated at 1200 watts requires 10 amps. A typical 100-amp house circuit allows you to draw 100 x 120 = 12,000 watts, often called 12 Kw (a Kw, or Kilowatt, is 1000 watts).

Anchor Bolt

Steel bolt used to secure the wooden sill pate to the foundation wall.

Appraisal

An estimate of the value of anything. Merely because a house is "professionally appraised" at $100,000, it is not necessarily worth that. Another appraiser — even a professional one — might "appraise" the house at $80,000. The value of the house is determined by what the seller can get for it: an appraisal merely gives him an idea of a starting point.

Asphalt

This is a thick, sticky mineral derivative, very much like a thick tar, which is used for waterproofing shingles and for "blacktop" driveways. It may also be used to coat roofs. Solid at normal temperatures, it may soften in extremely hot sun.

Astragal

This is one of those wonderful words that only homebuyers ever learn. It is the moulding, attached to one of a pair of double doors, against which the other door strikes when it closes.

Backfill

After foundations have been laid, the earth that was excavated is tamped back hard around them. This earth, which is used to fill the hole back in, is logically called "backfill."

Balloon Framing

This was the usual method of framing before about 1490, when PLATFORM FRAMING replaced it. It is distinguished by the long studs which run from the SILL PLATE all the way up to the roof. It is less fire-resistant than the newer form of framing.

Balusters

Uprights supporting the hand-rail on the outside of stairway. See also BALUSTRADE and NEWEL POST.

Balustrade

Hand-rail or guard-rail alongside a stairway or on a landing (or outside, beside any drop, for that matter).

Beam

A beam is a main structural element, which may be used to support floor JOISTS, RAFTERS, and other lesser parts of the frame. Traditionally wood, beams are now most commonly steel girders.

Bearing Wall

Load-bearing wall, supporting a floor or a roof. Piercing a bearing wall (for a door or window, for example) usually requires careful reinforcement of the structure; piercing (or even tearing down) a PARTITION WALL will not affect the structural integrity of the house. Of course, you need to know which walls are structural (bearing) walls, and which are not, *before* you start tearing them down.

Bevel Siding

Another (and more descriptive) name for CLAPBOARD.

Binder

Also known as a *binding option*, this is a contract between a buyer and a seller. The buyer gives the seller a sum of money (effectively a deposit) which secures for the buyer the right to buy the property at the agreed sum.

Bleaching Oil   If your redwood or cedar SIDING or deck is not weather fast enough to suit your taste, bleaching oil will speed the process up. Many people think that natural weathering looks better.

Blisters   Blisters in paint are usually caused by painting onto wet, oily or improperly prepared surfaces. The blisters will soon pop, and when they do, water can get in. Blisters on roofs are generally caused by weathering, and are every bit as undesirable as blisters on paint.

BOCA   Stands for "Building Officials and Code Administrators International, Inc." Publishes a model building code.

Brace   A brace is a timber framing member, installed at an angle between two other timber members to brace or stiffen the structure.

Brick Facing   Sometimes, brick is used almost as a SIDING: a thin brick wall, only one brick thick, is attached to the wall SHEATHING by metal ties.

Brick Veneer   The same as BRICK FACING

Bridging   Usually, two pieces of timber arranged in a flattened cross (like a railroad warning sign) and placed in a vertical position between two JOISTS to brace them and to distribute the load on them.

Bridging Loan   If you buy one house before you have sold the previous one, you may need a bridging loan to finance the old house until you sell it. Normally, bridging loans are financially crippling and should be avoided, but if the value of property is "spurting" as it sometimes does, you can actually profit from a bridging loan. One of my friends saw the value of his "old" house go up by $50,000, during which time he paid less than $5,000 in bridging loan interest. He sold it at the new, higher price, too!

Building Code

Building codes may be local, city-wide, county-wide or statewide (or, for that matter, federal). Most of them make sense, because they prohibit dangerous building practices, but some (such as declaring a chipped sink a violation of the building code) make you understand Davy Crockett's approach to house-building: he moved further west whenever he could see the smoke of another man's chimney.

Building Line

(also called "setback") The distance from the ends or sides of the building lot, beyond which building may not extend. The building line may be established by COVENANT, by BUILDING CODES, by ZONING ordinances, or by the filed subdivision plan.

Building Permit

Legal permission (from local government) to build according to agreed-upon plans. A building. that was constructed without a permit may, in extreme cases, have to be torn down.

Cantilever

A BEAM, TRUSS or slab is said to be cantilevered when it extends beyond its support. For example, a diving board on a swimming pool is cantilevered.

Cap

A stone or concrete cover to prevent the ingress of rain, for example on top of a brick chimney.

Casement Window

A casement window is hinged along one side, and opens like a door.

Casing

The technical building term for door and window frames.

Cavity Wall

A cavity wall is nothing more or less than a wall with two "skins" and a cavity or space in between. In this country, cavity walls are normally of wood, but brick cavity walls and cavity walls using mixed materials (cinder-block and brick, for example) also exist.

Cement

Strictly, "cement" is anything that is used to stick other things together. In building work, it is usually Portland cement. This is a "hydraulic" cement, made by calcining limestone with chalk; when it is mixed with water (hence "hydraulic"), it will set solid.

Certificate of Title

A certificate of title is issued by a title company as a result of a TITLE SEARCH. It says that the seller has good TITLE to the land and is entitled to sell it.

Change Order

All requests for changes in construction should be made in writing, to avoid subsequent disputes about who ordered what, and when, and how many changes there were. These requests in writing ar called change orders.

Circuit Breaker

A circuit breaker is akin to a fuse, in effect if not in design. When an electrical circuit is overloaded (i.e. when you try to draw more CURRENT through it than is designed for it), the circuit breaker snaps open and breaks the circuit, thereby removing the risk of overheating. Unlike a fuse, which has to be replaced, a circuit breaker can be reset like a switch.

Clapboard

Clapboard is wooden siding consisting of long, slightly wedge-shaped planks — one edge is thicker than the other. When it is being nailed up, the thicker side goes downwards.

Closing Costs

These are the costs of "closing" or completing the sale of a house; they are also called completion cost. They include attorneys' fees, apportionment of utilities and taxes, etc.

Closing Day

Also known as "completion day": the day on which the sale of the house is closed, completed or made final.

Cock Loft

Space between the ceiling and the roof, in a flat-roofed house. Usually only a couple of feet deep.

Collar Beam

This is a horizontal beam connected to two rafters, usually around half-way up, to "tie them together" and resist their natural tendency to spread outward. If it is installed lower, at or near the bottom of the rafters, it is called a TIE BEAM.

Column

A column is a vertical support, with one end usually on the ground and the other holding up a BEAM, PORTICO or roof. See also LALLY COLUMN.

Commission

Percentage paid to real estate broker in return for his work. Varies enormously, from about 1 percent to 10 percent. It is paid by the *seller*, not the buyer.

Concrete

Concrete and CEMENT are *not* the same thing. Concrete consists of sand, gravel or small stones (or all three) bound together with cement and water.

Condensation

All air contains moisture; that is what we call "humidity." Cool air can hold less moisture than warm air, so if warm, moist air is cooled (for instance, on a window pane or a cold wall), the water condenses out and stays on the cooler surface.

Conduit

Conduit or conduit tubing is metal piping designed to route, hold and protect electrical wiring.

Contract

A contract is a legally enforceable agreement which requires three components: an offer, an acceptance, and "consideration." "Consideration" means "something given in exchange," and it does not particularly matter *what* is given in exchange. For example, if I offer to buy your house for one dollar, and you accept my dollar, the contract is legal. Unless there are special provisions to the contrary, a verbal contract is every bit as binding as a written one.

Coping

"Coping" is the name given to the tile or stone caps that protect the top of a masonry wall (or the edge of a swimming pool) from water ingress.

Cornice

A decorative projection at roof level which overhangs the side of a building. Classical cornices were of stone, or sometimes of wood; modern ones are of wood, metal, or even plastic.

Counter Flashing

Counter flashing is let into brickwork on a parapet wall or other wall intersecting with a roof; it overhangs the FLASHING and prevents water entry. See Figure A, page 30.

Courses

A horizontal row of bricks in a wall.

Covenant

A restriction on what you may or may not do with the building, including additions, alterations, and even use. Will usually be uncovered by the TITLE SEARCH. Covenants may be personal, amounting to agreements between the present owner and his neighbor, or they may run with the land, so that you get the benefit (or otherwise) of the covenant if you buy the house.

Crawl Space

A low, unfinished area under the floorboards, usually accessible from the cellar or basement.

Cripple Studs

These are short wooden framing members that are used to support the frame of a window or door.

Current

Current is a measure of the power available from an electric circuit: the lower the current rating, the less power is available. It is measured in AMPS (Amperes). If you try to draw more amps from a circuit than it can handle, one of three things will happen. The circuit breaker will trip; the fuse will blow; or, if there is no circuit breaker or fuse, some part of the circuit will overheat and quite possibly start a fire. Now you see why circuit breakers and fuses are so important.

Damp Course

A damp course is a waterproof layer in a brick or other MASONRY wall, which prevents water moving upward from damp foundations.

140

Deed

A legal document that sets out the transfer of real estate.

Depreciation

Depreciation is largely a fiction in real estate, though the IRS allows buildings to be depreciated (i.e. reduced in value to reflect wear and tear) just like other property. With real estate *appreciation* (increase in value) is much more usual.

Double Glazing

Literally, a window or door which is glazed with pairs of panes of glass, with a sealed insulating space between each pair.

Double-Hung Window

A vertically sliding window, with both the upper and lower SASHES suspended on cords or chains with counterweights.

Drywall

A type of interior wall sheeting, typically applied in sheets 4' x 8'. Often called "sheetrock" though this is actually a brand name for a particular variety of drywall.

Easement

An easement is the legal right to make limited use of land belonging to someone else; for example, the right to pass across the land.

Eaves

The projection or overhang of the roof beyond the walls of the house.

Efflorescence

Stains on brickwork or concrete, caused by moisture penetrating the surface and leaching out minerals inside the material. When the moisture returns to the surface and evaporates, the minerals deposits are left behind as white or dirty-white stains.

Encroachment

A building is said to encroach on another person's property when it extends beyond the property line within which it should have been built. The same term is also used when a building extends past the BUILDING LINE.

Encumbrance

Property is "encumbered" when anyone has a right of action against it which diminishes its value — though the diminution in value may be large or small.

Engineered Fill

If earth is properly compacted, it becomes very much more predictable in its engineering or structural qualities than common or "garden" dirt. Properly compacted earth is sometimes called "engineered fill."

Equity

Take the market value of the property, "free and clear." Subtract any MORTGAGES, LIENS, or other debts. This is the "equity" that the property owner has. For example, a $100,000 house with a $60,000 mortgage means $40,000 equity.

Escrow

Funds are held "in escrow" until potential problems have been resolved: TITLE SEARCHES, the writing of contracts, or whatever. The escrow company (or the lawyer holding them in escrow) will pay these funds to the seller if there are no problems, or return them to the buyer if there are any problems.

Fascia

A fascia (or fascia board) is a flat, non-structural building member that covers a section of eave or (more rarely) cornice. Rainwater gutters are attached to the fascia.

Fill-Type Insulation

Also known as "loose insulation." This is insulation which can be poured or blown into a space, as distinguished from roll-type insulation. Some types of insulation are not only more effective than others, they are also much more resistant to vermin.

Fire Box

The fire box is the combustion chamber in a boiler or furnace.

Fire Brick

Fire bricks are special high-temperature bricks (sometimes call "refractory bricks") that are used to line fire boxes.

Fire-Stop

"Stop" is a misnomer: all that most "fire-stops" do is to slow the spread of smoke and flame by dividing the interior of a PARTITION WALL or other CAVITY WALL into smaller spaces. they are usually made of 2"x4" lumber.

Flashing

Flashing is traditionally made of zinc or lead, though you may encounter galvanized metal or even plastic flashing. Its purpose is to protect the junctions between roofs and vertical structures (parapet walls, chimneys, etc.) and prevent water entry. See also COUNTERFLASHING.

Floor Joists

See JOIST.

Flue

A "chimney" to allow the smoke and fumes produced by a boiler, furnace, wood fire, etc., to escape to the outside.

Flue Liner

Clay lining material used inside brick chimneys to protect the brickwork; usually available in two-foot-long section of either round or square section.

Flue Pipe

A metal flue.

Footing

The underpinning of the foundation wall, usually of poured concrete in modern houses.

Foundation	The masonry or concrete base on which the house is built. Most of it is out of sight below the GRADE LINE, but some of it must protrude above the earth so the wooden walls will not be in direct contact with the moist ground.
Foreclosure	If a MORTGAGOR (person receiving a loan against a house as security) fails to pay debt installments, the MORTGAGEE (whoever makes the loan) is entitled to seize the property in satisfaction of the debt. This is normally only done as a last resort.
Framing	"Framing" is the construction lumber used to build a frame — wall STUDS, RAFTERS, JOISTS and the like.
Frost Line	The frost line is the depth to which frost can penetrate the soil. FOOTINGS are normally placed below the frost line.
Fuse	A fuse is designed as the "weak link" in an electrical circuit. When the circuit is overloaded, the fuse melts, thereby breaking the circuit. In the United States, most fuses are of the screw-in type.
Gable	Gable roofs have a steep PITCH, and usually imply large, spacious attics.
Gambrel	A gambrel roof has two different PITCHES, one on each side of the RIDGE BOARD.
Grade Line	The grade line is the soil (dirt) level against the wall of the house.
Grade Markings or Grade Stamp	Construction lumber is graded for quality, whether or not the wood is KILN DRY, and

the type of wood. Grades number 1 and 2 are acceptable for load-bearing members; Grade 3 should be reserved for members which bear only their own weight (i.e. not JOISTS, RAFTERS, etc.).

Grantee
The grantee is the person to whom the property is "granted" or sold.

Grantor
The grantor is the person who "grants" or sells the property.

Header
A header is a framing member which sits atop the SILL PLATE; the FLOOR JOISTS are attached to it.

Hose Bibb
A fancy name for an outside faucet.

Jamb
A jamb is the wood (or more rarely, metal) frame that surrounds a window (window jamb) or door (door jamb). It is sometimes called a CASING rather than a frame.

Joist
A joist is a transverse framing member used to support a floor (floor joist) or roof (roof joist).

Kiln Dry
Traditionally, wood was "seasoned" by leaving it to age naturally. This is almost unheard of for modern construction lumber, which is normally dried in a heated kiln to give a moisture content of six to twelve percent. Kiln dry timber is less likely to warp than "green" or fresh lumber, but it is more prone to warping than properly seasoned wood.

Knee Wall
A knee wall is a short framing member used for wall construction in attics. It runs from the RAFTER to the JOISTS, and rather resembles a slightly bent knee in appearance.

Lally Column	Lally columns are round steel pillars used to support BEAMS or JOISTS. They should be concrete-filled.
Leader	This is the technical term for what most of us would call a down spout — a drain that carries water down from a roof gutter.
Lien	A lien is a legal right to recover money, chargeable against a piece of property. In extreme cases, a lienholder can force a sale in the same way that a MORTGAGEE can (see FORECLOSURE.
Lintel	A lintel is a transverse structural member across a flat-topped window or door. The traditional material was stone; modern lintels are mostly steel.
Load-Bearing Wall	See BEARING WALL
Masonry	Masonry is the craft of constructing walls of stone, brick, or other permanent building blocks.
Moisture Barrier	A moisture barrier is placed between a damp area (e.g. earth) and a dry area, for obvious reasons. Moisture barriers in modern houses are mostly either plastic or metal foil.
Mortgage	A mortgage is a loan which is made with certain types of property (in most cases, real estate) as security for the loan. If loan payments are not made, the mortgagee (the person or institution granting the mortgage) has the right of FORECLOSURE against the mortgagor (the person having TITLE to the property against which the loan is made).

Newel Post	The newel post is the main post at the foot of the staircase which anchors the hand-rail or BALUSTRADE.
Non-Bearing Wall	See PARTITION WALL.
Nosing	This is the rounded edge of a stair TREAD which protrudes over the RISER.
On Center or Between Centers	The spacing of studs, joists and so forth is measured (logically enough) from the center of one stud to the center of the next. Equally logically, the measurement is given as "on center" or "between centers," so "twelve inches on center" or "twelve inches between centers" means that the middles of the members are twelve inches apart. Because of the thickness of the members, the gaps between the member will be smaller: with two-inch-wide members, for example, the gap will be 10 inches if the members are twelve inches on center.
Partition Wall	A partition wall, sometimes known as a "party wall" or just as a "partition," is an interior wall which is of no structural importance; it is not a BEARING WALL.
Pitch	"Pitch" is a measure of the angle or steepness of a roof. Steeply pitched roofs shed water and (especially) snow more efficiently than gently pitched roofs, but they are heavier and more expensive to build.
Plaster	Plaster is a mixture of lime, sand and water that provides a smooth interior finish — though plaster may also be applied "rough cast" for special effects (restaurants do this a lot!)

Platform Framing

Most modern houses use this style of framing, which is more fire-resistant than BALLOON FRAMING. Each stud wall is only one story high, with the studs attached to the SOLE PLATE and the TOP PLATE.

Points

Mortgage lending rates can vary widely. Normally, there is, at any one time, a "standard" or "prime" rate, to which "points" (percentages of the amount of loan, in one percent increments) may be added by the lender. "No points" mortgages are more usual when money is freely available and the lender has no reservations about either the borrower or the property.

Pointing

"Pointing" is the neat finishing of the mortar between COURSES of brickwork. If the mortar is uneven or just bulges out any old way, the wall is unlikely to be well built. See also REPOINTING.

Post and Beam

"Post and beam" construction, most often seen in barns and other farm buildings, uses heavy posts as upright members to support BEAMS, instead of using JOISTS and STUDS.

Principal

MORTGAGE repayments consist partly of interest, and partly of money which reduces the amount owned. The amount actually owed is the principal.

Putty

Traditional putty consists of a mixture of linseed oil, but there are other "putties" which may be made of other ingredients.

Radiant Floor Heating

"Hot floors" are accomplished by embedding water pipes or electric heating elements in concrete or by laying such pipes or heating elements between a sub-floor and a finished floor. They are *very* expensive to repair, as the whole floor usually has to be ripped up. Some "hot floors," though, consist only of electrical heating laid under a carpet — rather like a room-sized electric blanket.

Rafter

Strictly, a rafter is a structural member which runs from a wall to a RIDGE BOARD, though the term is often used loosely of COLLAR BEAMS, TIE BEAMS and even roof JOISTS.

Refinancing

Sometimes, it is advantageous to take out a second loan against the house, and clear the first one. This may be because of a fall in interest rates, to extend the repayment period of the MORTGAGEE, or (more usually) to make money available for improvements, extensions or other purposes. Refinancing usually takes advantage of the rise in the value of the property since it was bought, which results in the owner having greater EQUITY.

Repointing

As a brick or MASONRY wall ages, the mortar between the bricks (the POINTING) may crumble. Periodically, therefore, the old mortar should be scraped out to a depth of half an inch or so, and replaced; this is repointing.

Ridge Board

This is the "peak" of the roof, like the ridge-pole of a tent. The RAFTERS are attached to it.

Riser

The riser is the vertical section of a step in a staircase.

Rock Wool

Rock wool is an insulating material similar to fiberglass. Also called "mineral wool" and "slag wool," it is made from stone and molten slag. It has a high melting point and is inedible, though vermin may still use it to build nests.

Roofing Felt

Roofing felt is a felted (fibrous) material impregnated with asphalt. It comes in rolls.

Roofing Paper

See ROOFING FELT.

Sash

The "sash" of a window is the bit that holds the glass — the inner frame, if you like. The outer frame is called the JAMB or CASING.

Septic Tank

In areas where there is no mains drainage, sewage is normally discharged into a septic tank. There, it is broken down by bacteria and soaks in to the earth via a leaching bed.

Shakes

Shakes are hand-cut shingles — or sometimes, shingles that are machine-made to look as if they were hand cut.

Sheathing

Sheathing is the external covering of the frame of the house; it is typically plywood in sheets eight feet by four feet.

Shingles

A shingle is a small piece of slate, wood, or synthetic material which is applied in a series of overlapping layers as SIDING or roofing.

Siding

Siding is the outermost covering of a building. CLAPBOARD siding is traditional; vinyl and aluminum siding are common; and SINGLED siding is also found.

Sill Plate

The sill plate is the first wooden framing member, attached directly to the

FOUNDATION wall with ANCHOR BOLTS.

Sistering

A beam, joist or other wooden structural member is "sistered" when it is reinforced by having member bolted or clamped to it for reinforcement.

Skirt Board

A skirt board is an angled structural member which is secured to wall STUDS to support the TREADS and RISERS of a staircase.

Soffit

Only home buyers and carpenters have ever heard of this word! it is the underside of the eaves.

Sole Plate

A sole plate is the bottom wood member of a framed stud wall and rests on the SILL PLATE.

Solid Bridging

Because joists are typically quite thin compared with their depth (two inches as against eight or ten inches), they are sometimes prone to twisting. A solid bridge is a short piece of wood placed between the joists, usually at the center of their span, to remove any tendency to twist.

Special Assessment (Special Tax)

Sometimes a local authority will levy an extra tax to pay for a particular project — road construction, sewer installation, sidewalks, street lighting and so forth.

Splash Block

A splash block is a piece of MASONRY or CONCRETE placed under a down-spout or LEADER to divert water away from the house to a place where it cannot harm the foundations.

Stringer	The "stringer" is the support of the "outside" end of a staircase. The TREADS and RISERS are supported by the stringer at one end and by the SKIRT BOARD at the other. Needless to say, a stringer is a long, strong piece of wood.
Stud	A stud is an upright structural member used for wall framing, usually a two-by-four.
Sub-Floor	This is another term which is largely self-explanatory: it is the plywood sheeting attached to the JOISTS, over which the finished floor is laid.
Suspended Ceiling	In old buildings with high ceilings, you will sometimes find suspended false ceiling that are hung from the original ceiling. The two main reasons for installing them are to reduce the volume that has to be heated, cooled or ventilated, or to restore the proportions of a room that has been divided in two and therefore has a disproportionately high ceiling. They may also be installed to provide a convenient space for installing hot-air or air conditioning ducts.
Termite Shield	Termites can't cut through metal. Metal sheeting therefore discourages them wonderfully. Termite shields are made of thin metal.
Tie	A tie (or tie beam) is a horizontal member running between two rafters, at or near the bottom of the rafter. It literally "ties" the two rafters together and stops them spreading apart, as well as reducing the outward pressure on the walls. Roofs that are covered with heavy roofing materials (such as slate)

are more likely to need tie beams than others with lighter coverings.

Title

In the legal sense, "title" usually means one of two things. The one you are most often concerned with is easy to understand: if you hold title to a piece of land, you are entitled to keep it. The "title" that you hold is a legal document which states that you are the owner (or sometimes possessor) of the land. The other use of "title" is as a description of a particular piece of legislation: for example, building codes might be "Title 1234" (or whatever) of your local state's legal code.

Title Insurance

After the TITLE SEARCH, the title search company or the lawyer conducting the title search will guarantee that the SELLER holds good TITLE and may sell the property — but they will also buy title insurance in case they are wrong! In many states, this title insurance covers *only* the title itself, but you can buy additional insurance against LIENS or other ENCUMBRANCES which were not discovered. Such additional insurance is a good idea.

Title Search

This is a legal investigation which checks that the SELLER actually does own the house and is entitled to sell it. The title search should also turn up any other ENCUMBRANCES, but see TITLE INSURANCE. Exactly who conducts the title search will vary from state to state.

Top Plate

"top plate" is a misleading term, as there is no "plate" involved at all: these are long, horizontal members which make up the top of a framed wall. To make it still more confusing, they are often called a "double top plate." The roof rafters and ceiling joists are supported by the top plate.

Tread

The tread is the flat bit on each stair, the part you step on. The vertical bit is the RISER.

Trap

A U-trap is a simple way of preventing sewer odors from getting into the house. The "U" is always filled with water, and thereby isolates the sewers from the house.

Truss

A truss is a complete assembly of rafters, joists and braces, sometimes prefabricated, usually triangular in shape and used in roof construction.

Valley

This is yet another self-explanatory term: it is where two sloped roofs meet, or where a sloped roof meets a parapet wall.

Vapor Barrier

A vapor barrier is akin to a MOISTURE BARRIER but is specifically intended to stop CONDENSATION. Where a vapor barrier is used in conjunction with insulation (as it normally is), it should be placed with the insulation on the *cool* (unheated) side of the vapor barrier.

Vent Stack

The vent stack is a pipe, connected to the main drain, which rises above roof level to vent sewer gases to the atmosphere.

Vermiculite

Technically, a "laminated hydrous silicate"; in practice, a sort of puffed-up mica which is very light and makes wonderful FILL-TYPE INSULATION.

Volts

A measure of the "pressure" of electricity. Standard American wiring is around 120 volts. In most of the rest of the world, the "pressure" is higher at between 220 and 250 volts. Because higher voltages are more efficient and can convey more power (see WATTS), appliances with a high power consumption (such as clothes dryers or small space heaters) are usually 220 or 240 volts in this country.

Wall Sheathing

See SHEATHING.

Watts

A measure of the power consumed by an electrical appliance. A telephone answering machine might use only 100 watts; a powerful electric water heater might use 7000 watts (7 kilowatts, or Kw). See also AMPS, VOLTS.

Weep Hole

A small hole in a MASONRY or CONCRETE wall that allows moisture to drain away from behind the wall.

Zoning

Different areas may be "zoned" for residential use, light industrial use, agricultural use, etc. Infringement of zoning regulations can be quite a serious offense. If the house you are inspecting seems to be out of character with the rest of the area, check that it complies with zoning regulations — either ask the owner, or call City Hall.

CHECKLISTS

All of the checklists on the following pages are designed either to be answered "Yes" (just put a checkmark in the space provided) or "Not Applicable" (N/A) — for example, if the house you are looking at does not have wooden siding, you just write "N/A" beside the questions on wooden siding. Only when you get a "no" or "don't know" answer is there any reason to worry.

For your convenience, photocopy a full set of checklists for each building you look at. You can then compare the checklists at your leisure, or use them to brief a professional building inspector when you find the house that you want.

Please note: these checklists are summaries of the reset of the book. **They are not a substitute for reading it**. This is why I have "keyed" each checklist section to the relevant section in the main body of the text.

CHECKLIST 1 — EXTERIOR

WALLS AND SIDINGS (Section 2.1 — pages 22-28)

Are the walls free from bulges? ___

Is the pointing sound? ___

Is the wall free of cracks? ___

Is wood siding straight? ___

Is wood siding sound? ___

Is the paint good? ___

Are shingles sound? ___

Is metal or vinyl siding okay? ___

Is there insulation board behind siding? ___

Is the stucco sound? ___

ROOFING (Section 2.2 — pages 28-35)

Is the roof steep enough to shed snow? ___

Are there any slates/tiles/shingles missing,
    damaged or misplaced? ___

Are there fewer than three layers of
    synthetic shingles? ___

Are asphalt paper roofs bubble-free? ___

Is the flashing sound? ___

Are coping stones or tiles sound? ___

GUTTERS AND DOWNSPOUTS (Section 2.3 — pages 35-37)

Are gutters complete and well fastened? ___

Are down spouts complete and connected? ___

Do downspouts direct water away from the foundations? ___

WINDOWS AND DOORS (Sections 2.4 and 2.5 — pages 38-46)

Do windows open and close easily? ____
Are there any rattles? ____
Is there any wood rot? ____
Are sash-cords sound? ____
Is the paint good? ____
Is the putty sound? ____
Are the windows double glazed? ____
Are double-glazed windows free of condensation on the side? ____
Do doors open and close smoothly? ____
Are there any rattles? ____
Does the door look secure? ____
Is the door double blazed? ____
Are there storm doors? ____
Are the door and window locks good? ____
Are there grilles and/or shutters? ____
Can you get *out* easily in an emergency? ____

CHECKLIST 2 — INTERIOR

FOUNDATIONS (Section 3.1 — pages 48-56)

Are the foundations free from cracks?   _____
Are there any signs of repairs to the foundations?   _____
Are the foundations dry?   _____
Are the foundation walls free from bulges?   _____
Are the foundations free from efflorescence?   _____
Are skirting boards neat and in place?   _____
Are stairs "true" and well fixed to the wall?   _____

LOAD BEARING STRUCTURES (Section 3.2 — pages 56-60)

Is the house of platform-frame construction?   _____
Are the timbers sound?   _____

ROOF (Section 3.3 — page 60)

Is the ridge-board sound?   _____
Are the rafters sound?   _____
Is there any water damage below roof level?   _____

FLOORS (Section 3.4 — pages 61-63)

Are the floors of wood?   _____
Are the joists sound?   _____
Are the joists 16" or less between centers?   _____
Are the joists big enough?   _____
Are the ends of the joists sound?   _____
Do the floors feel solid and springy?   _____
Are any joists "sistered"?   _____
Are the lalley columns concrete filled?   _____
Are the floors insulated?   _____

ACCOMMODATIONS (Section 3.5 — pages 63-67)

Is the plaster sound in every room? ____
Ar all rooms free from water damage? ____
Is the drywall sound? ____
Do the rooms suit your lifestle? ____
Is there enough privacy? ____
Are the fireplaces well-built and lined? ____
Is the chimney free of creosote build-up? ____
Do you have to walk through any of the
rooms to get to any other room? ____

BATHROOM (Section 3.5 — pages 67-68)

Are the bathroom fixtures in good order? ____
Do the bathroom faucets and drains work? ____
Is the toilet sound in working order? ____
Is water pressure in the shower satisfactory? ____

KITCHEN (Section 3.5 — pages 68-70)

Are the kitchen fixtures in good order? ____
Do the faucets and drains work? ____
Does the kitchen suit *your* lifestyle? ____
Is kitchen cooling and ventilation adequate? ____
Are there adequate means of escape from the house
in case of fire? ____

GARAGES (Section 3.6 — pages 71-72)

Is there enough storage space? ____
Is the garage floor sound? ____
Are the garage walls sound? ____
Is the garage adequately fireproofed? ____
Does the garage door operate freely? ____
Is the garage door in good order? ____

ATTICS (Section 3.6 — pages 72-73)

Is the attic vented? ____
Is the attic insulated? ____
Is there a vapor barrier? ____

CELLARS AND BASEMENTS (Section 3.6 — 74-75)

Is the cellar above the water table? ____
Is the cellar free from water stains? ____
Is the cellar free from musty smells? ____

CRAWL SPACES (Section 3.6 — page 75)

Are crawl spaces accessible? ____
Is there a vapor barrier between the earth and
the floorboards? ____

OUTBUILDINGS (Section 3.6 — pages 75-77)

Were the outbuildings constructed with building permits? ____
Are the outbuildings sound? ____

CHECKLIST 3 — SYSTEMS

WATER (Section 4.1 — pages 80-84)

Is there a main water supply?
Is the system delivered through COPPER pipes? ____
Is there a *working* mains shut-off valve? ____
Is there a drain valve? ____
Are the pipes installed in a way that minimizes the risk of freezing? ____

Are the water heater and the central heating boiler separate? ____
Is the water heater 50 gallons or bigger? ____
Is the water softener ecologically acceptable? ____

DRAINAGE (Section 4.2 — pages 85-86)

Are the drain pipes sound?
Is the drainage system vented? ____
Do drains empty quickly? ____
Is the septic tank trouble-free? ____

ELECTRICITY (Section 4.3 — pages 86-90)

Is the power supply at least 100 amps?
Is the wiring professionally installed? ____
Are there enough power outlets? ____
Is all wiring of copper (not aluminum)? ____
Are electrical appliances in good order? ____
Does electrical heating work? ____

GAS (Section 4.4 — pages 90-92)

Is gas installed?
Are gas appliances in good order? ____
Is the gas furnace in good order? ____

OTHER SYSTEMS (Section 4.5 — pages 92-95)

Is there a telephone installed?   ____
How many telephone outlets are there?   ____
Is the TV reception good?   ____
Is the TV aerial sound?   ____
Is cable TV connected or available?   ____
Is there any kind of security system?   ____
Is it efficient?   ____
Is it reasonably free from false alarms?   ____
Are smoke detectors fitted?   ____
Are fire sprinklers fitted?   ____

INSULATION (Section 4.6 — pages 95-97)

Are the heating bills acceptable?   ____
Is the roof well insulated?   ____
Are the walls well insulated?   ____
Is there good underfloor insulation?   ____
Are vapor barriers correctly installed?   ____

HEATING (Section 4.6 — pages 97-100)

Is the heating furnace reasonably modern?   ____
Was solar heating professionally installed?   ____
Is the house heated by hot water or hot air?   ____
Is the central air conditioner fairly new?   ____
Is the air conditioning correctly installed?   ____

CHECKLIST 4 — OUTDOORS

YARDS (Section 5.1 — pages 104-113)

Does the yard/garden suit your lifestyle? ____

Is it clear who owns the land around the house? ____

Do you like the landscaping? ____

Are there any dangers in the garden? ____

Will you have time to maintain the garden? ____

Are trees sound and well clear of the house? ____

Is the yard free from dead wood? ____

Are paths and driveways free from "heaves" caused by roots? ____

Are paths and driveways in good repair? ____

Are any paths built over access covers? ____

Are steps safe (including handrails)? ____

Are retaining walls in *excellent* condition? ____

Has the property the benefit of any rights
of way or easements? ____

Is the property free from any rights of way or other
obligations to others? ____

PORCHES, PATIOS AND DECKS (Section 5.2 — pages 113-117)

Is the woodwork/metalwork sound? ____

Is the area free from vegetation underneath? ____

Is the patio level and smooth? ____

Are the edges of the patio sound? ____

Is the sun room adequately ventilated? ____

POOLS AND HOT TUBS (Section 5.3 — pages 117-119)

Is the pool in conformity with building codes,
and has it the necessary permits? ____

Is the structure of the pool sound? ____

Was the plumbing installed by a licensed plumber? ____

Was the pool wiring (including the pump)
installed by a licensed electrician? ____

Is the hot tub (or jacuzzi) in good order? ____